CU00405238

Book Cover

Photo by Irene Reid

Enhanced by Prisma Photo Editor

Potted history

Town Charter

The little village of Bilbao was given Town status and vital market rights by Don Diego Lopez, the Lord of Biscay in 1300.

The little town soon expanded into what is now called the "Seven Streets", Bilbao's Old Town.

Expansion

By the 16th century Bilbao had cornered the export trade of Merino wool from Castile, and was shipping it to Northern European cities like Antwerp.

Trade boomed and Bilbao was soon exporting all sorts of Spanish goods to the rest of Europe. It became the most important commercial and financial hub on the Northern coast.

They even shipped to England - in Hamlet, Shakespeare wrote:

"Methought I lay worse than the mutines in the bilboes."

The bilboes mentioned being leg shackles imported into England from Bilbao.

Industrial Revolution

Bilbao was perfectly placed at the start of the industrial revolution and soon became a major player in mining, steel, and shipbuilding.

Of course, Spain went through several upheavals over the centuries.

Bilbao was besieged four times during the Carlist Wars., which were basically a civil war between two claimants to the Spanish throne in the nineteenth century.

On one side was Don Carlos, who was the brother of the deceased king. His side fought for the status quo. On the other side was Princess Isabella, the three-year old daughter of the king. Her side were Liberals who fought for change. The wars lasted for forty years.

Bilbao was on the side of the Liberals and was never conquered - as is proudly recorded in the city's title "The Undefeated Bilbao".

Bilbao later expanded across the river, got its university near the end of the nineteenth century, and by the start of the 20th century Bilbao was the wealthiest city in Spain.

Spanish Civil War

Later the Spanish Civil War erupted. That was a battle between those fighting for a democratic republic, and the army lead by General Franco who were ultra conservative. Bilbao was on the Republican side, so didn't fare well after the war. However Franco needed the money from Bilbao's industry, so the city again expanded rapidly to meet the demand. Franco finally died after forty years of dictatorship and like the rest of Spain, Bilbao started to live again.

Flood and modernisation

In 1983 disaster struck when the city was completely flooded by the river. Many people lost their lives and a huge amount of damage was done. They rebuilt and cleaned up, but the city fathers were determined to move away from heavy industry. They embarked on a modernization project which was centred on light industry and tourism; what you see today is the result.

Shipping is still important and Bilbao is still one of Spain's busiest ports. These days however the docks have been moved down-river to the bay, as the river cannot be navigated by today's enormous container ships.

Get ready to explore

Bilbao Card

Before you travel, you should check if the Bilbao card is going to save you money and time. Details can be found at:

https://www.bilbaobizkaiacard.com/en/home/

Guggenheim Day

Next, check if there is a Guggenheim "free day" during your visit before you start to explore it. If there is, you may want to avoid it because there will be incredibly long queues to get in - mostly locals. You will find it much more fun if you can just buy your ticket and walk in when it's quieter.

Fog Sculpture and Fire Fountain Timetable

Fog Sculpture and Fire Fountain are art works which sit outside the Guggenheim Museum and which generate special effects.

They both kick off at specific times of the day. You can find out the timetable from the Museum when you visit, or from the tourist office.

Town Hall

If you want a guided tour of the Town Hall to see the Arab Hall (see page 33), you need to book in advance. You can write to:

girpa@alcaldia.bilbao.net

Opening Hours

Be aware of Bilbao opening hours and plan your walks accordingly. In general public buildings, and that includes churches, are open in the morning, shut early afternoon, and re-open in the late afternoon.

Foods to Try

Pintxos

As you explore Bilbao you will come across many bars and cafes selling pintxos - a Basque specialty. They are delicious little one-bite snacks, usually a piece of bread with a delicious topping, or perhaps a tiny skewer of meat.

They are quite different to tapas which you get in the rest of Spain, and which are often just a slice or scoop of a much larger pot of food – e.g. tortilla.

Make sure you try them at least once!

Salt Cod

If you are a fish eater you will want to try the fish specialty, Bacalao al pil pil. Salt cod is cooked in a sauce of oil, garlic, and cayenne pepper.

Something Sweet

Finally if you are having a coffee and fancy a cake to go with it, try one of Bilbao's specialties:

First there is the Pastel Vasco, sometimes called the Gâteau Basque. It's a slice of tart which is usually filled with vanilla or almond flavored cream, although you can find fruit-filled versions.

The Carolina is a pastry topped with meringue and chocolate.

Finally the Jesuita de cabello de ángel is a triangle of puff pastry filled with sweet pumpkin.

The Walks

The walks actually join up. So if you have the energy and time after finishing one walk, you could start another.

There are three walks to enjoy:

Walk 1 - Guggenheim to the Arenal Bridge. 3.5 km

Walk 2 - Old Town. Shortest Route 3 km

Walk 3 - Arenal Bridge to the Museum of Fine Arts. 3 km

If you can, tackle Walk 2 on any day from Tuesday to Friday. Those are the days when you will find the Seven Streets at their liveliest, and the huge Mercado will be open.

The Maps

Each walk starts with an overview map, just to give you an idea of the route.

There are detailed map sections sprinkled through each walk to help you find your way.

If you need to check where you are at any point during a walk, always flip back to the previous map to find where you are.

To help you follow the maps each map shows its start point. In addition numbered points have been placed on each map. The number points correspond to the numbered directions within the walks.

Street Names

The street-signs of Bilbao normally have the street-names in both Spanish and Euskara, the language of the Basques.

Make sure you have a look at the lovely street-signs. The signage is in a traditional Basque form of lettering from ancient inscriptions on gravestones. It's been turned into a type face called Harri which means stone in Basque.

Walk 1 – Guggenheim to the Arenal Bridge.

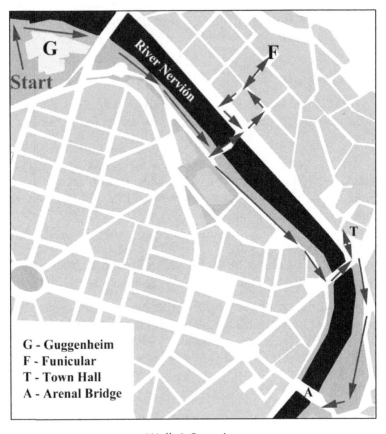

Walk 1 Overview

This walk first takes you around the Guggenheim Museum, followed by a pleasant stroll along the river-side to reach the edge of the old Town.

It includes the possibility of a short trip on the funicular, up into the hills to see Bilbao from above.

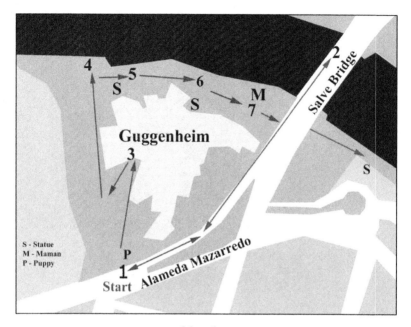

Map 1

The walk starts on Alameda Mazarredo, just outside the grounds of the Guggenheim Museum of Modern Art. Puppy stands guard at the entrance.

Puppy

Almost as eye-catching as the museum itself, is Puppy, the twelve meter high West Highland terrier which stands guard outside the Guggenheim.

Puppy is carpeted in flowers. He was designed by American Jeff Koons and even has his own internal irrigation system to keep those lovely flowers in perfect condition. The locals call Puppy, El Poop.

Just before the grand opening of the Guggenheim museum, police officer Jose Maria Aguirre spotted and tried to intercept several ETA terrorists who were disguised as Puppy's gardeners and were trying to plant bombs in the flowers. They claimed that the museum was imperialistic! Sadly Aguirre was shot and killed in the shoot-out that followed.

Movie Link

Puppy also makes an appearance in the opening sequence of "The World is not enough". Bond escapes from a window and you can see Puppy as he drops to the ground.

> If you need the tourist office, stand face-to-face with Puppy and turn left. It's in the little stand-alone office in front of you.

The Guggenheim

In the eighties, the city fathers embarked on an ambitious program to ignite interest in their city. They planned to build an airport, a subway, and a new bridge across the river. But even more ambitiously, they planned to build an international art museum to bring the tourists into Bilbao.

They approached the Guggenheim Foundation and after many, many meetings, the Guggenheim was coming to Bilbao.

They knew that they needed something really spectacular to house the museum, so a competition was announced – and the plans that the winning architect Frank Gehry put forward were certainly eye-catching.

The museum is sited in the old industrial heart of Bilbao and the design reflects the city's ship-building history. It is built of limestone, glass, and titanium. When finding the building materials they had problems finding the right limestone, but eventually located it in Andalusia, down in the South of Spain. It's said that the building does not have a single flat surface.

If the sun shines it will light up the Titanium to a golden colour. Of course it rains a lot in Bilbao – but with luck you will see it gleaming.

If you view the Museum from the right angle, it resembles a huge gleaming ship.

The New York Times described it as:

> A fantastic dream ship of undulating form
> in a cloak of titanium.

Map 1.1 – Cross the road to Face Puppy and turn right.
Walk up the gentle slope onto the striking La Salve Bridge.

Salve Bridge

The bridge's real name is The "Princes of Spain" Bridge.

"Salve" is a prayer to the Virgin Mary, and it gets that nickname because Basque sailors coming back into port would catch their first glimpse of the Basilica of Begoña high above Bilbao. They would say a prayer giving thanks to Mary for their surviving another voyage.

The Salve Bridge's colourful red arch was added as a celebration of the tenth anniversary of the Guggenheim. The "Red Arches" project won the design competition, as the judges liked the softening of the approach to the Guggenheim, compared to the previous heavy iron arch which it replaced.

The designer Buren said:

> "You see the museum as soon as you come onto the bridge, and I liked the idea of the viaduct structure being covered with a deep red arch, through which vehicles and pedestrians would have to pass to get in and out of Bilbao. As if it were a huge open door connecting the city with the rest of the world.

When you are about halfway over the bridge, turn round to see the Guggenheim as it's meant to be seen. It really does look like the last ship built in Bilbao, sitting on the river Nervion.

Movie Link

James Bond walks over the Salve Bridge with the Guggenheim in the background, as he makes his escape in the opening sequence of "The World is not enough"

Map 1.2 – Make your way back over the bridge and return to face Puppy.

Walk down the slope and steps to approach the museum entrance and venture in. Even if you don't like modern art, the museum itself is fun to explore.

Inside the Guggenheim

Eleven thousand square meters of exhibition space are distributed over its nineteen galleries.

Now, modern art either thrills you or puzzles you, and how you feel will dictate how long you spend exploring the museum itself.

Many people enjoy exploring the interior of the building as much as the artworks to be found there. It's a bit bewildering as there seems to be endless stairs, walkways, and corridors to follow as you explore this museum.

As you do, here are some interesting, if puzzling, pieces to spot:

Installation for Bilbao - Jenny Holzer

This installation is near the entrance and is quite fun. It's a row of nine LED floor-to-ceiling columns, which illuminate phrases in Basque, Spanish and English.

The Matter of Time - Richard Serra

This is a huge artwork and it is in the largest gallery. It is essentially a set of huge iron constructions of various shapes which you can enter and walk through. As you do the rusty orange coloured walls around you will bend, lean over you, twist and turn, and then straighten up again.

Some people experience disorientation when exploring them, perhaps you will too.

Wish Tree for Bilbao – Yoko Ono

This is an olive tree. At times the museum invites visitors to tie a tag to the tree with a special wish on it.

Untitled - Mark Rothko

It's the big yellow and red rectangle!

Rothko is one of the best known modern artists. He is famous for paintings like this one, of coloured rectangles which are said to represent human emotions. This one

16

doesn't have a real title – Several of Rothko's works are left Untitled.

It is huge, so that when you look at it you see nothing else. The suggested distance for viewing is just 18 inches away. Rothko is quoted as saying:

> "Small pictures since the Renaissance are like novels, large pictures are like dramas in which one participates in a direct way."

Large Blue Anthropometry - Yves Klein

It's the big blue splodge!

The artist made use of what he called "living brushes" – naked paint-covered females pressed their bodies onto the canvas and voila, a "masterpiece".

Sunflowers - Anselm Kiefer

This is very different from Van Gogh's joyful painting.

The artist has painted a naked man at the bottom of his painting, and above him towers a field of dark, dying sunflowers.

The Renowned Orders of the Night - Anselm Kiefer

This is another painting by the same artist. No sunflowers this time, just the stars in a dark sky above another prostate figure.

One Hundred And Fifty Multicoloured Marilyns - Andy Warhol

Why have just one Marilyn when you can have so many more?

Alchemy – Jackson Pollock

Jackson Pollock is one of the few modern artists that most people will have heard of – even if they've never see any of his work. His paintings sell for millions.

He was one of the fore-runners of "Abstract Expressionism". His technique was to place a canvas on the ground and then run around it or over it with a paint can, dripping lines and splodges onto it as he did – this was called the drip technique. Some of his paintings have footprints on them. He gained the nickname "Jack the Dripper". Make of the result what you will.

Composition 8 - Vasily Kandinsky

This was painted a few years after World War 1. No splodges this time - you can actually make out circles, triangles, and other geometric shapes.

Kandinsky had a theory on the emotional properties of shapes and colour. This painting is a kind of shape dictionary, where each coloured shape projects an emotion of some sort. You are supposed to feel those emotions when looking at the different shapes.

Food Stop

If you need refuelling after exploring the Guggenheim, the bistro on the ground floor of the museum does very good pintxos, those delicious little Basque snacks.

Map 1.3 – When you exit go back up the steps, but then turn right to reach another set of steps which will take you down towards the river.

Map 1.4 - Turn right at the bottom of the slope so that the river is on your left and the Guggenheim is on your right.

Pause after a few steps to find the artwork "Tall Tree and the Eye".

Tall Tree and the Eye

This work of art by Anish Kapoor consists of 73 gleaming spheres built into a tree which is fifteen meters in height.

The spheres reflect the surrounding city, the river, the bridge, and each other as you walk past them. They are supposed to remind us of the instability of our view of the world.

Try zooming in on one of the spheres to get an interesting snap!

Map 1.5 - Continue along the riverside until you spot a large colourful bunch of tulips, also on your right.

Tulips

You can't miss Jeff Koons's Tulips which add a bit of colour and cheerfulness to the back of the Guggenheim.

Koons's theme when he designed them was Celebration. You probably saw them in much closer detail when you explored the inside of the museum, as from there you have access to the platform they are sitting on from the main atrium

Fog Sculpture

If you time it right you will see a mist emerge from the pool of water in front of the Tulips. You can find out the timetable either at the museum or at the tourist office. It changes depending on the season.

The mist is a piece of modern art, by Fujiko Nakaya called Fog Sculpture.

Fire Fountain

Again if you time it right, you will see the fire fountains, which are on small platforms in the water. This is another piece of modern art, by Yves Klein.

Klein did not want a mass of colour, unlike Koons, so the colours are quite muted, pale blue, gold and pink.

Map 1.6 – Continue towards the red arch of the Salve Bridge. You will be greeted by Maman as you do.

Maman

In contrast, Maman is the rather scary spider sculpture lurking behind the Guggenheim. It's by artist Louise Bourgeois who became the best-paid living woman artist, all thanks to her lovely spiders; they sell for millions.

This one is amongst the largest sculptures in the world standing over 30 feet high and over 33 feet wide and she is carrying 26 marble eggs. Maman represents motherhood, by spinning, weaving, nurturing, protecting and it is clearly compelling.

Map 1.7 - Continue along the Riverside walking under the Salve Bridge. You will pass another huge red arch.

Pause when you reach a statue of a suited man with hands in his pockets. It's on your right.

The Door of the honourable

It is a statue of Ramon Rubial and he is walking towards The Door of the Honourable.

Rubail was an ardent socialist who fought on the Republican side in the Spanish Civil War against Franco. For this he was sentenced to thirty years in prison, and he spent nineteen years there before being freed.

He immediately returned to politics, becoming the senator for Biscay in the first democratic elections in 1977. He died in Bilbao.

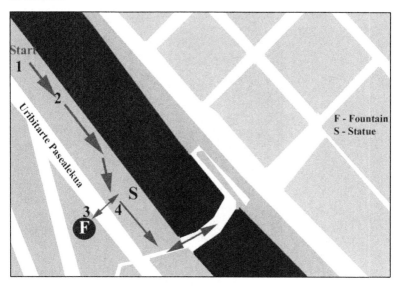

Map 2

Map 2-1 - Continue along the riverside.

It is a pleasant stroll along the river Nervion. Try to imagine what it was like when the riverside was full of shipyards and workers.

Map 2.2 - The pathway you are on will split after about 200 metres.

Take the right-hand upper pathway and then use the nearby zebra crossing to cross Uribitarte Pasealekua to reach a fountain.

Melpomene

The fountain is decorated with a statue of Melpomene holding a lyre. She is the muse of Singing and Tragedy and the daughter of Zeus.

This statue once stood outside the Museum of fine Arts. It was a replacement for the museum's original naked statue of Melpomene which was deemed far too daring and was stashed away for 27 year in the vaults.

When the original naked Melpomene was finally rescued and reinstalled outside the museum, this Melpomene was relegated to this location near the river. You will see the original statue on Walk 3 which visits the Museum of Fine Arts.

Map 2.3 - Return to the river-side and turn right to continue. A little further along you will come to Las Sirgueras.

Las Sirgueras

This is a powerful statue which shows four women of Bilbao, using ropes and raw strength to haul barges packed with goods upstream to the old town.

Sand sometimes blocked the estuary and stopped large boats reaching the city. When that happened, the goods were unloaded onto barges and Las Sirgueras, the women, got to work.

No-one, man or woman, would do that kind of work unless they had to, and the women involved had to. Their men were either fighting in the wars or dead, and they had to support their children.

Their efforts were not appreciated and the women were vilified for doing it. Perhaps their accusers felt shame that the women were reduced to doing it and that it was even allowed.

One newspaper of the day said:

> "Is there no way to avoid this sad and disgusting spectacle that continues to offer itself to our eyes?"

Their story had mostly been forgotten, perhaps deliberately. But it has been rediscovered and this statue pays tribute to their work.

Map 2.5 – Continue and you will reach the Zubizuri footbridge.

Climb the steps and make your way halfway over the bridge to see the city from the river.

Zubizuri Bridge

It was designed in the shape of a sailboat and it is paved in glass. The glass was very controversial; the main problem being the number of people who slipped in the rain and fell while trying to cross the bridge.

Eventually Bilbao put its citizens' safety above the architect's feelings, and covered the central pathway over the bridge with a non-slip material.

Optional Funicular Diversion

You might like the idea of a funicular ride up into the hills behind the buildings on the other side of the bridge. It takes less than five minutes to get up there and it's very cheap.

If that idea doesn't appeal to you, continue this walk from "End of Funicular Diversion" on Page 32.

Otherwise to reach the Funicular:

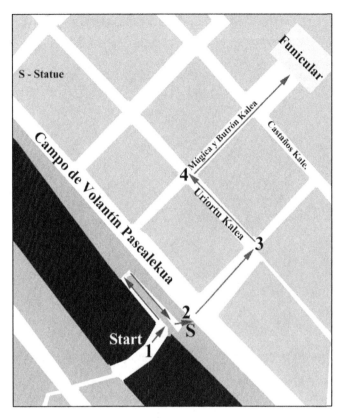

Map 3

Map 3.1 - Cross the Zubizuri Bridge.

From the bottom of the steps turn right and a few steps will bring you to a striking statue.

Hombre vence al hierro (Man defeats Iron)

This statue is by local artist Jesus Lizaso.

Here is the man, straining every muscle and stretching his neck backwards, as he fights to bend the piece of metal in his hands.

The artist has greatly exaggerated the man's features to dramatise the moment – just look at those enormous hands and feet.

To the Funicular

Map 3.2 - Cross busy Campo de Volantín Pasealekua using the zebra crossing just next to the statue.

Once over, go straight ahead into pedestrianised Epalza Kalea.

Map 3.3 - You will reach a crossroads with Uriortu Kalea where you turn left.

Map 3.4 - Take the next right into Múgica y Butrón Kalea.

At the end of Múgica y Butrón Kalea walk straight ahead into Plaza del Funicular. You will see the funicular station ahead of you.

Buy a ticket and enjoy the ride up. When you exit the station follow the pathway to the left. It will take you to a viewing spot where you can enjoy the view of Bilbao.

While you are there, do take a look at Huella Dactilar.

Huella Dactilar - Juan José Novella

It is a huge fingerprint. It is a memorial to the victims of the Spanish Civil War and it was only installed in 2006.

The fingerprint represents the mark and impression which all the victims of that war left behind on their families, friends, and on Basque society.

When you are ready to move on, make your way back to the station and take the funicular down the hill.

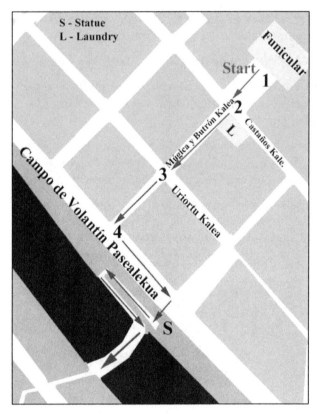

Map 4

Map 4.1 – Once down, exit the funicular station and walk across Plaza del Funicular. Pause at the crossroads.

Castaños Laundry

On the left-hand corner in front of you is an unexpected modernist building – don't miss the sweet little flowers which adorn the windows. The architect studied in Barcelona and his work was influenced by the modernist buildings he found there.

It was built in 1910 and incredibly it originally housed a laundrette! Bilbao had been badly hit by cholera in the nineteenth century, so the council had laundrettes built around the city.

This one was later converted into a market and then expanded to operate as a civic centre. You can see the much more modern building stuck on top of the original building. It does look totally out of place.

Map 4.2 – From the crossroads, continue straight ahead along Múgica y Butrón Kalea.

Map 4.3 - Cross Uriortu Kalea. Continue along Múgica y Butrón Kalea to return to the riverside.

Map 4.4 - Turn left to return to the Zubizuri Bridge and climb up the steps.

End of Funicular Diversion

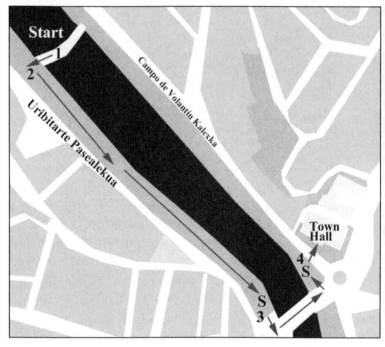

Map 5

Map 5.1 - Re-cross the bridge and make your way down the steps to return to the river-side.

Map 5.2 – Turn left to walk with the river on your left-hand side.

You now have a five minute stroll along the riverside to reach a modern statue which stands near the next bridge. It's called Day at the Sea.

Day at the Sea

This statue celebrates the joys of the beach. Walk around it and you will see that it does look like a child enjoying the feel of the sea-breeze blowing hard against him.

Map 5.3 - Go up the steps behind the statue to reach a much larger bridge. Cross it and turn left to find another modern statue.

Oval-Shaped Variant of the Sphere's Idleness - Jorge Orteiza

What a title!

Apparently this statue explores ways of constructing things based on linearly twisted curves. More understandably, it's made of weathered steel and represents the long-gone shipyards of Bilbao which once lined the river.

Map 5.4 – Carefully cross the road which runs along the riverside to reach the Town Hall.

Town Hall

Before this Town Hall was built, the council met in a building which stood next to the San Anton church - you will see the church on Walk 2.

That Town Hall had been flooded by the river more than once, so the council decided that a new Town Hall was needed and built it on a much grander scale.

It was constructed on the site of an old San Augustine Convent. The convent had been turned into a fortress during the Carlist Wars, and destroyed by bombs.

At the top of the wide stairway you can see two ten foot marble statues representing Law and Justice. The four chaps which you can see on the outer corners of the facade represent four local heroes; one is Don Diego Lopez of course, who founded Bilbao in 1300.

City Hall Interior

Inside the highlight is the Arab Hall. Its interior was painted to look like ivory, marble, and wood and it imitates the style of the Alhambra Palace in Granada.

You can get a guided tour of the Town Hall, but you must book it well ahead of your trip.

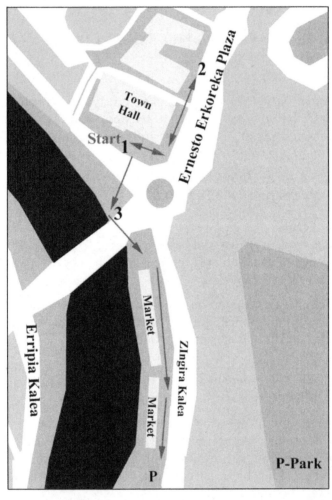

Map 6

Map 6.1 – Face the Town Hall and then walk down the right hand side.

You will reach the much more modern and state-of-the-art City Hall which sits behind the Town Hall. It's eye-catching, but not nearly as handsome as its parent.

Map 6.2 - Return to the bridge but don't re-cross it.

Map 6.3 - Instead turn left and stroll along the river-side.

You will pass two markets where flowers and fruit/veg are sold most days. On Sunday it becomes more interesting, when collectors of stamps, coins etc. set up their stalls.

You will reach the edge of the Arenal Park.

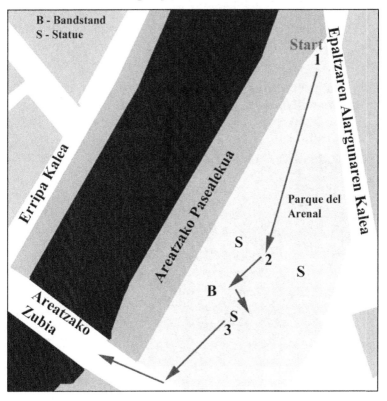

Map 7

Arenal Park

This little park holds maples, acacias, chestnuts and even a lime tree. It's a pleasant place to take refuge from the sun on a hot summer's day.

Map 7.1 – Walk through the park to reach the middle where you will find some fountains and statues

Pan and Bacchus

Among the trees are statues of Bacchus and Pan. Bacchus is the god of wine so he is holding a bunch of grapes in his hand, and leaning on what look like a vine.

Pan is the god of the herds. Here he is playing his flute and has what looks like an animal skin slung over his shoulder

Map 7.2 – Continue a little further. On your right-hand side, you will find a lovely Art Deco bandstand.

The Bandstand

Don't miss the pretty stained glass windows at the back of the bandstand stage, and the carvings on the roof above them. Then stand back a bit to see the two cherubs on the

roof – They stand on pillars which are also covered in decorative carvings.

If you visit on a bank holiday or a Sunday you might hear the Bilbao Symphonic Orchestra playing to an appreciative audience. Even if there is no show on, it's a lovely bandstand and well worth a look.

Just in front of the bandstand you will see a statue of Balendin Enbeita.

Balendin Enbeita

Balendin Enbeita was an author, but is most famous for being one of Bilbao's best bertsolaris. They are poets whose skill is to quickly compose a poem, put it to a tune, and then sing the result to their audience. Balendin founded the first bertsolari school in 1958.

The tradition started long before that and is very much a part of Basque culture. The bertsolaris perform at key social events like weddings, funerals, and christenings.

There are also many competitions where large audiences gather to watch them out-sing each other. The biggest competition is held once every four years in the Basque country. The competitors are given a topic and a tune, and have just two minutes to create a poem and sing it to the tune.

Balendin is carved in a very natural pose, wearing a jacket and a cap, as though he is about to perform.

Map 7.3 – Continue to the end of the park. Turn right to reach the Areatzako Zubia (Arenal Bridge).

You have now reached the end of this walk.

You could continue with Walk 2 which takes you through the Old Town and starts from this bridge.

Walk 2 – Old Town

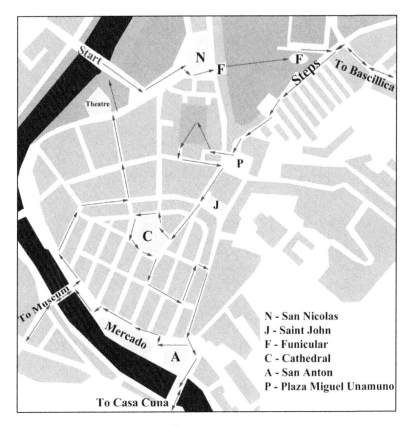

Walk 2 Overview

This circular walk takes you from the Arenal Bridge into Bilbao's old town before returning you to the Arenal Bridge.

There is an optional side-trip of going up the hill which sits above the Old Town (by funicular!). There you can visit Bilbao's most loved church, the Basilica de Begoña.

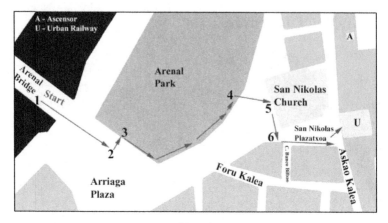

Map 1

This walk starts on the Arenal Bridge.

The Arenal Bridge

Face upstream. On your left is the old town and on the right is the Abando district.

Abando was originally a separate town, but as Bilbao grew it expanded beyond the old town and over the river to absorb Abando. Clearly a bridge was needed to join the two communities up.

The first bridge erected on this spot was made of iron and was built in the mid-nineteenth century. It could be raised to let boats through and it was named Isabella II after the queen. At that time anyone crossing the bridge had to pay a toll.

Eventually the bridge fell apart thanks to age, war, and flooding. It was replaced by a stone bridge which was also called the Isabella II. It was destroyed during the Spanish Civil War in 1937.

This bridge was built in 1938 and was named the Victory Bridge, but it was renamed in 1980 to Areatzako Zubia, the Arenal Bridge.

Map 1.1 – Cross the bridge towards the Old Town.

Map 1.2 - Use the zebra crossing on your left to reach the edge of the Arenal Park.

Map 1.3 – Turn right to skirt around the edge of the park.

Map 1.4 – Stop when you reach the front of the San Nicolas church on your right. Use the zebra crossing to reach it.

San Nicolas

Saint Nicolas de Bari is the patron saint of sailors, so the riverfront of a maritime city is a very appropriate setting for the church.

San Nicolas History

When the first church was built here, the area in front of it was just a sandy beach where the fishermen landed their catch. It was the fishermen who first built a little chapel in honour of Saint Nicolas on this spot.

As Bilbao expanded the little chapel grew into a church. Sadly it was destroyed in the sixteenth century by one of the many river floods

This church was built in the eighteenth century, and was again dedicated to Saint Nicolas. Like many churches it has had a chequered history. It's been hit by lightning and used for various military uses, but has now been restored.

1983 Flood

Spot the oval plaque to the left of the door, marking where the water reached in the flood of 1983 - nine inches of rain fell in just one day. The plaque is well above head height.

It was after the devastation of that flood that Bilbao began its revival, and reinvented itself as a cultural city.

San Nicolas Exterior

You can see that it's quite an austere church with two towers topped with crosses.

Saint Nicholas and the Fishermen

Above the main door, two lions hold a shield of Bilbao's coat of arms between them. The coat of arms has a church on it, but it's not this one. You will read about San Anton later in the walk.

Below the lions is a bronze bas-relief by Josep Limona whose works can be seen all over the world. It depicts Saint Nicholas and the fishermen.

If the church is open, do go in to have a look around.

San Nicolas Interior

It's a beautiful octagonal church with a wide white dome spanning the church.

The five altars and the pews are all made of dark walnut and were recently restored. So when you enter the church you are struck by the contrast of the dark wood against the white stone.

When Bilbao built this church they wanted it to stand out so they commissioned Madrid's best artists to design and build the altarpieces.

The High Altar

You will immediately be drawn to the high altar where Saint Nicholas stands in the centre niche, high above you and is surrounded by gleaming gold.

Saint Nicholas

At Saint Nicholas's feet are three little children coming out of a barrel. They allude to the saint's most famous miracle.

Three children were abducted by an evil butcher who killed them, cut them up, and put the body parts into a salting barrel to be sold as hams.

Sometime later Saint Nicholas appeared at the butcher's door and demanded that the barrel be opened. He prayed to God and the three little children rose out of the brine, whole and well.

Not surprisingly Saint Nicholas became the patron saint of children and we now know him better as Santa Claus.

Saint Vincent and Saint Lawrence

The two figures in red robes which stand on either side of Saint Nicholas and holding palm leaves are Saint Vincent and Saint Lawrence.

Above each is a painting of their martyrdom, Saint Vincent was beaten to death and Saint Lawrence was roasted to death. Saint Lawrence famously told his torturers:

> "I'm well done on this side, turn me over"

In both paintings you can see a golden ray of light travelling from heaven marking each man as a saint.

Altarpiece of the Pietà

The Pieta is a name given to statues where Mary holds the body of her dead son, and you can see one here. It is taken out of the church on Good Friday and joins the procession around Bilbao.

Don't miss the bas-relief on the altar which shows sinners suffering in the flames of purgatory. One sinner has been purified and an angel is hauling her up to heaven.

Altarpiece of San Blas and Sore Throats

This is one of the most popular altars in Bilbao. To understand why, you have to know the story of San Blas.

He was a doctor who became Christian and headed off to live in a cave as a hermit for a while. His most famous miracle was saving the life of a child who had a fishbone stuck in his throat. You can see this miracle depicted above the statue of San Blas.

So now on the saint's day in February, stalls appear on the plaza outside the church selling doughnuts and "cords of San Blas".

After eating their doughnuts, the faithful put the cords around their necks and come to this chapel to get the cords blessed by San Blas. They pray to the saint to protect them from a sore throat. They then must wear the cord for nine days and then burn it to complete the deal.

You can see the proceedings here:

https://www.youtube.com/watch?v=qhSBGWCjYPw

Map 1.5 –When you exit the church, turn left and cross San Nikolas Plazatxoa.

Map 1.6 - Turn left to walk down San Nikolas Plazatxoa passing little Calle Banco Bilbao on your right. San Nicolas will be on your left-hand side on the other side of the street.

As you approach the end of San Nikolas Plazatxoa, you should spot the towering Ascensor de Begoña on your left.

Ascensor de Begoña

It's a lift which opened in 1915 and gave easy access to the high hill in front of you. The lift carried its passengers up to a high walkway which passengers would walk across to reach the hillside.

It was only shut three times in almost a hundred years. Once during the Civil War when it was bombed and inoperable. Once after an accident which although serious, did not result in any deaths. And once after the disastrous flood of 1983, when mud and debris slid down the hill and buried the station.

The rickety old lift was finally closed in 2014. Bilbao is now trying to decide what to do with the Ascensor in the future.

At the end of the street you will see the entrance to the urban railway station ahead of you. It contains the funicular which is the replacement for the Ascensor de Begoña.

You now have a choice.

You can take the new replacement funicular up the hill to visit the Basilica de Begoña. The walk from the upper station to the Basilica takes about ten minutes each way. Then you can descend the hill via a long flight of steps.

The Basilica de Begoña is Bilbao's most loved church and is dedicated to the city's patron saint, the Virgin of Begoña.

Many would say it is worth the effort to see it, but if you are short on time or energy you may prefer to give it a miss.

Staying Down?

If you wish to skip the Basilica, you can just walk straight to the bottom of the steps which you would have used to come down the hill, and continue this walk from there.

To do that:

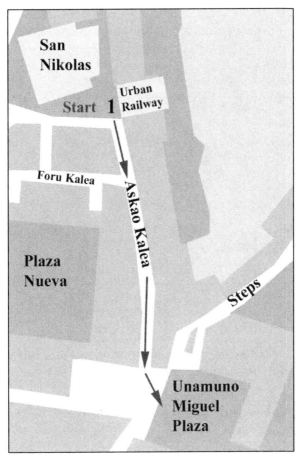

Map 2

Map 2.1 – Face the railway station in front of you. Turn right to walk along Askao Kalea for about 150 meters.

You will reach a busy little square on your left which is called Unamuno Miguel Plaza.

The walk should only take you about three minutes. The steps which you could have come down are on your left.

Once in the square, re-join the walk from "The Elements" on page 61.

Going Up?

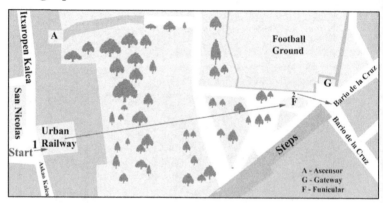

Map 3

To go up the hill and visit the basilica:

Map 3.1 - Enter the station in front of you and buy a ticket to take the funicular up to Begoña.

Map 3.2 – Exit the funicular station at the top and turn right. Walk slightly uphill and you will reach the corner of Bario de la Cruz.

Gateway and Bilboes

As you reach Bario de la Cruz, you will see a stone gateway with four pilasters on your left. The gateway has been incorporated into a wall which runs around Mallona Football ground.

Take a look at the top of the stone gateway where you will see an engraving. On the far left is something which looks very like the bilboes mentioned by Shakespeare in his play, which you read about in the Potted History.

Bilboes consisted of two U shaped iron hoops which were threaded onto an iron rod. A prisoner's feet were put through the hoops and the rod tightened, making it impossible to take a step.

On your right you will see the long flight of steps which you will use to get back down the hill later.

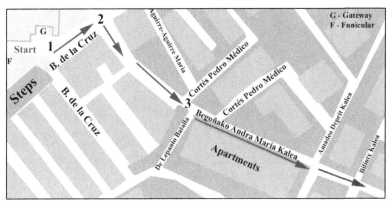

Map 4

Map 4.1 – With the long flight of steps behind you, walk straight ahead along Bario de la Cruz.

Map 4.2 – Take the first right into Begoñako Andra Maria Kalea.

You are now walking through the La Salve district. If you have already done Walk 1 you will remember that Salve is the nickname of the bridge next to the Guggenheim.

51

It was the Basilica de Begoña tower, high on the hill, which returning sailors first spotted returning from dangerous voyages.

You will reach De Lepanto Batalla Kalea on your right, and from that point you can see the Basilica tower in the distance.

Map 4.3 – Continue straight ahead. Walk past the high apartments on your right and head towards the Basilica.

Pass Amadeo Deprit Kalea and Bilintx Kalea on your left. The street you are following will become pedestrianised.

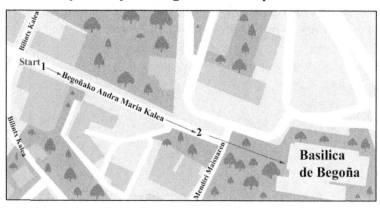

Map 5

Map 5.1 - Follow the pedestrianised street and climb several short flights of steps.

Map 5.2 - Make your way towards the front of the Basilica.

Basilica de Begoña

You can see the Basilica's clock tower from quite a way back – it holds 24 bells all constructed in Switzerland.

As you get nearer you will see the enormous triumphal arch enveloping the main door.

Look above the rather plain door to see a sculpture of the Last Supper. The experts tell us that Judas sits in the group to the left of Jesus, grasping a bag of silver.

It is actually a copy of Leonardo da Vinci's Last Supper which is in the Santa Maria delle Grazie church in Milan:

Da Vinci's The Last Supper

The Legend of the Basilica

This Basilica was built where a carving of the Virgin Mary is said to have appeared in the sixteenth century.

There are a few legends about the appearance of the Virgin Mary carving. The most popular tells us that a shepherd found a carving of the Virgin on a tree branch and built a little hermitage to put it into.

Worshippers wanted to move the carving into a new shrine in another location, but the Virgin was having none of it. The carving rooted itself into the ground and a voice called

Bego oina!

a phrase which has been interpreted as meaning "Stay". So the people built their new shrine in the same place instead.

The statue was given the name Begoña from the words "Bego oina", although the faithful also call it "Amatxu" which means Mother.

Basilica History

The first church was later built where the shrine stood. The church was started at the end of the sixteenth century, but has had several additions and alterations over the centuries to reach its current size and grandeur. Again, like most large churches, it suffered various indignities and setbacks through the centuries.

When Napoleon arrived in Spain the army looted the church and caused great damage.

The tower was blown up by the Carlist army thirty years later. In 1836 the church was stripped of combustible items, including the altarpiece, as Bilbao stood against another attack by the Carlists. They used it as fuel. The tower was attacked once again in the Third Carlist war in 1850 and was rebuilt in 1881. It was rebuilt one final time in the twentieth century and so far has survived.

The church has now been restored to its former glory. Each year on the day before Assumption Day, thousands of pilgrims climb the hill and walk to the Basilica to attend midnight mass.

It's also where the local football team, Athletic Bilbao, walk to barefoot while singing at the start of the season to leave flowers and pray for success.

Inside the Basilica

Go in and sit on a pew to look up at the beautiful vaulted ceiling which is held up by towering columns. The way the ceiling is decorated makes the columns look almost like trees.

You should examine the high altar to see the simple wooding carving which was found so long ago.

There is also a nice courtyard to visit and perhaps rest your feet for a while.

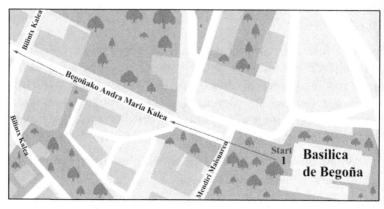

Map 6

Map 6.1 - Once you have explored the church, return to the main door and face away from it.

Walk straight ahead and go down the steps. You will reach Bilintx Kalea on your right.

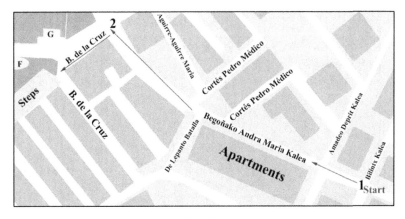

Map 7

Map 7.1 - Continue straight along Begoñako Andra Maria Kalea all the way back to the T – junction with Barrio de la Cruz.

Map 7.2 - Turn left along Barrio de la Cruz to return to the top of the long flight of steps.

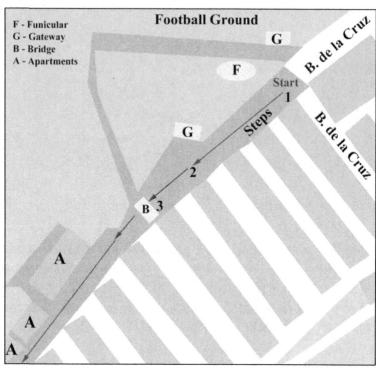

Map 8

Map 8.1 – You will see there are actually three paths leading downhill. Take the middle one which has a railing on the right-hand side.

On the way down you will see another old gateway on your right.

Going Down

Gateway

At one time it was the entrance to an old cemetery. It is now part of the park which covers this hill.

Map 8.2 – Continue downhill and a little further down is sweet little stone bridge. It also gives access to the park.

Map 8.3 - Keep going down the steps. About halfway down the hill you will see some colourful apartment building with iron balconies on your right.

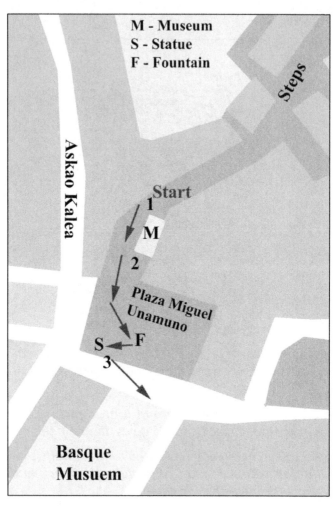

Map 9

Map 9.1 – The steps will swing left. Just before you reach the bottom you will find an iron fence and gate on your left.

That is the entrance to the Archaeological Museum which might interest you. If so, pop in. If not interested continue from "Reaching the Bottom" on page 61.

Archaeological Museum

It's a nice but small museum, so it won't take too long to explore.

The one downside to the museum is that all the exhibit information boards are in Spanish and Basque only, but you could buy a little guide book if needed.

The ground floor holds the oldest fossils, some almost half a million years old. Upstairs you will find more items, from the earliest human settlements, to Roman and Visigothic times, and finishing with the Middle Ages.

The museum's most popular relic is a set of pieces of a sailboat, which have been pieced together on a frame to show us what the boat would have looked like. The remains of the boat were found in the Bay of Biscay and it was built in the fifteenth century.

Exit the museum when you have had enough.

Reaching the Bottom

Map 9.2 - When ready to move on, descend the last few steps to walk into a busy little square which is called Plaza Miguel Unamuno.

The Elements

Near the middle of the square is a nice little fountain where four heads dispense water.

Each head is dedicated to one of the four elements, Earth, Fire, Water and Wind, or as the fountain says in Eursaka, Lurra, Sua, Ura, and Haizea.

Miguel Unamuno

The square is named after Bilbao's cleverest son who was born near this square. He was a philosopher, professor, and a novelist, but he was also intensely political and fell foul of the Spanish government over and over again.

He became professor at Salamanca University but was ousted because of his very vocal criticism of Primo de Rivera, who was Spain's dictator prior to Franco. Unamuno was shipped to the Canary Islands, but from there he managed to escape to Paris.

He returned to Spain in 1930, however he was just as critical of the Republican Government then in power, and famously told a reporter that the President:

"should commit suicide as a patriotic act"

You can imagine how well that was received. Unamuno was sacked from the University once more, and all streets which had been named after him were renamed. But at least he wasn't sent into exile again.

Franco came onto the scene and initially Unamuno supported him. However the tactics by Franco's men made Unamuno change his mind:

"Franco's army is waging a campaign against liberalism, not against Bolshevism. They will win, but they will not convince; they will conquer, but they will not convert."

Unamuno was placed under house arrest by Franco until his death.

You can see a bronze bust of him at the top of a tall marble column at the edge of the square. The bust is a replica of the original which was tossed into the river in 1999. It lay there for several months before being rescued, restored, and placed in the Mayor's office for safety.

Map 9.3 - Stand face to face with Miguel Unamuno and walk diagonally left to find the Basque Musuem (Euskal Musea) at number 4.

Basque Museum

The Museum sits inside what was once the Jesuit College of the nearby church, which you will visit later. The College was the first building to be built outside the old town walls.

The museum houses all sorts of items used by the Basque people over the centuries, which is probably of limited interest to most people really.

However it also hosts the Mikeldi Idol in the central courtyard, and it's worth seeing if you like really ancient artefacts.

If you have a Bilbao card you will get a discount, so decide if you would like to see it and if so, pop in and visit the courtyard.

Note, the entrance to the courtyard is through a glass door which is just past the desk.

Mikeldi

The experts tell us that Mikeldi dates from the Iron Age.

Interestingly, it might have been first discovered in the seventeenth century. In 1634 Gonzalo de Otalora from Seville wrote a book called:

The Geographic Micrology of the seat
of the noble merindad of Durango

and in it he claimed to have found:

"an idol in Miqueldi of monstrous shape and size representing a rhinoceros holding a very big globe between its feet. On it are incomprehensible etchings"

However that idol was left where it was, and appears to have been forgotten about.

Mikeldi was unearthed in 1896 near the ruined Hermitage of Mikeldi, so it could be the same idol that Otalora found.

It's thought to be a bull or a boar, and it may have been used in some sort of religious or magical ceremony. On the animal's back there are indeed some markings.

Whatever kind of animal it is, the symbols and the disc under it are a puzzle. You can postulate your own theories.

Before your move on, you might like to know that the lovely courtyard you are standing in was actually the cloister of the Santos Juanes church. It is just next door and you will see it soon.

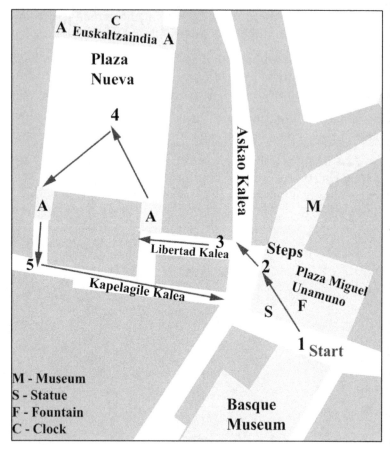

Map 10

Map 10.1 - When you exit the museum, cross the square diagonally left to reach the end of the steps railing.

Map 10.2 – Face away from the square and you will see two narrow streets in front of you. Take the right hand street which is called Libertad Kalea.

Map 10.3 - Follow it to reach an archway on your right which will take you into Plaza Nueva

Important - take note of which archway you entered by, so you can find your way out later.

Plaza Nueva (New Square)

This is a lovely neoclassical style square enclosed by arcades and arches, and with palm trees softening the setting with some greenery.

The square gets its name because when it was built Bilbao already had a Plaza Vieja or Old Square. That square has gone now but this one still remains New Square.

As you look around notice the difference in window size from the first floor to the top floor – it was more expensive to have a first floor residence with larger windows.

Regocijos

Long ago bullfights were staged in the square. Bilbao also once had a yearly festival known as the Regocijos. It's said that an old fountain which used to stand in the square delivered wine instead of water during the festival – that may or may not be true.

In 1872 King Amadeo I decided to attend the festival; so Bilbao pulled out all the stops in his honour. They transformed the square into Venice by flooding it, and locals dressed up as gondoliers and guided their gondolas across it. The city awarded a prize to the best gondola.

The Square Today

Nowadays the square is used for festivals and concerts, and has even hosted a Chess Grand Slam Masters final. If you visit on a Sunday you'll find a flea market which is fun to rummage around.

The arcades hold many taverns, restaurants, and gift shops, although it's very nice to just sit on the little wall at the edge and enjoy the atmosphere. It's a popular meeting place for the locals for some pintxos and txikitos - nibbles and wine to you and me.

The large building with the coat of arms and a clock at the top of the façade is the Euskaltzaindia – as it says just beneath the clock.

Euskaltzaindia

That is the Royal Academy of the Basque Language. The Basque name for their language is Euskara. The Academy staff work to ensure that Euskara doesn't die out like so many other minority languages.

They embarked on that task before the beginning of the Spanish Civil War. After the Civil war and under Franco's rule, the danger to the language increased and the battle to save Euskara was being lost. One key problem was the variants of Euskara which were spoken in isolated areas of the Basque region. Not having a single agreed language contributed to its decline – it's not a language if all the people speaking it can't fully understand one another.

The Academy pulled out all the stops to fully define the language. The new standard language was taken up by schools and for the moment Euskara seems to be safe, despite the continued reluctance of some people to give up their own versions.

Bar Bilbao

If you fancy a coffee or a pinxtos or two, you could take a look at Bar Bilbao which is beside the archway you entered the square by.

This is an old café which opened in 1910, and is decorated with many interesting prints, paintings and typically Spanish tiles.

Map 10.4 - When ready to leave the square, stand with your back to the Euskaltzaindia.

Opposite you and diagonally left is the archway which you entered by. Leave by the corresponding archway opposite you and diagonally right. It will take you out on Goikolau Cueva Kalea.

Map 10.5 - At the end of this little street, turn left along Kapelagile Kalea and you will return to the edge of Plaza Miguel Unamuno.

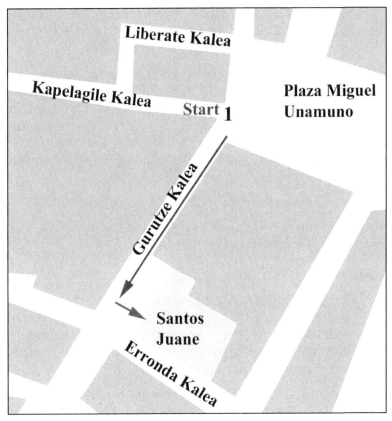

Map 11

Map 11.1 – Turn right immediately and you will walk into Gurutze Kalea.

Not too far down on your left-hand side, you will reach the Church of Joan Santuen.

Joan Santuen

This church is dedicated to Saint John – better known as John the Baptist. Its predecessor was dedicated to Saint Andrew and was founded by the Jesuits at the start of the seventeenth century . It was actually the church of the Jesuit College which sits just next door. Both the church cloister and the Jesuit College have since been converted into the Basque museum which you may have just visited.

The Jesuits only lasted 150 years in Spain, before being tossed out by King Carlos III in 1767. They became persona non grata in many of Europe's kingdoms at that time, as they were seen as wielding far too much power and wealth, and were too loyal to the Papacy for most monarchs' taste. However they managed to found Bilbao's University before that were expelled.

Saint Andrews church was rededicated to Saint John.

Go inside the church where you will find the walls lined with altars dedicated to various saints.

High Altar

The High Altar is straight ahead at the end of the nave. It is very ornate with masses of gold and four twirling Solomonic columns. The columns get that name, because in the Vatican there are similar columns, which are said to have come from the Temple of Solomon in Jerusalem.

John the Baptist is centre-stage on the altar since the church is dedicated to him. He is dressed in an animal skin so presumably it depicts him during his wilderness years.

To the left of him stands Saint Peter with his keys, and on the right stands Saint Paul.

San Luis Gonzaga Altar

This altar is on the left-hand side as you walk from the door down the nave.

Gonzaga was a young Italian nobleman who gave up his fortune to become a Jesuit priest. He was in Rome when the plague descended on that city, and he stayed to care for the sick. He died of that dreadful disease aged only 23.

The robe that Gonzaga's statue is wearing is beautifully sculpted, with soft folds in the cloth and wide flowing sleeves.

San José Altar

This altar is on the right-hand side as you walk from the door down the nave.

San José is better known as Joseph, Mary's husband. This statue is a modern replacement of the original which was lost in the 1983 flood. The artist has managed to replicate the softness of Gonzaga's robes.

Joseph is carrying a staff topped with white flowers – the flowers are said to be a symbol of his suitability to be the husband of the Virgin Mary.

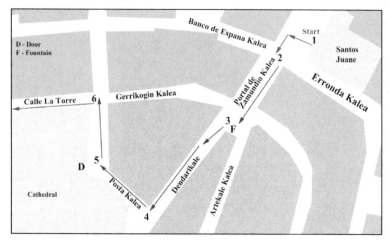

Map 12

Map 12.1 – Leave the church. Turn left but take just a few steps to reach a crossroads.

This is where the Portal de Zamudio once stood.

Portal de Zamudio

It was a gate in the old town wall which once circled the original Seven Streets of Bilbao. It was the only gate which gave access to the North, all the other gates in the wall gave access to the river.

The little street in front of you was named after the gate, and it is the shortest street in Bilbao.

Map 12.2 – Cross the junction and walk along Portal de Zamudio.

You will reach a fountain and behind it you will see a fork in the road.

72

Map 12.3- Take the street on the right-hand side of the fountain, which is called Dendarikale.

Seven Streets

You are now entering one of the Seven Streets, or the Siete Calles as the locals call them. This is the oldest part of Bilbao. The seven streets run parallel to each other and all lead down to the river.

The original three streets were called Somera, Artekale, and Tendería. Four more were built in the fifteenth century, and called Belostikale, Carnicería Vieja, Barrenkale, and Barrenkale Barrena. Each street was named to reflect the businesses found there.

The seven streets were all tucked safely behind the city wall which only came down in the sixteenth century to let the town expand.

Generation Gap

There is an ongoing argument between the older and younger residents of this part of Bilbao.

In the 1960's, local businessmen decided things needed modernising and took to calling their community the Old Town.

One of their arguments was that the "Old Town" had already expanded beyond the original seven streets, which is true enough.

Those who wanted to keep to the old name argued that there are "Old Towns" all over the country but only one "Siete Calles", which is also very true.

The arguments continue.

Map 12.4 - Take the first right, Posta Kalea. You will reach an ornate wooden double door as the street turns sharply right.

The Door of the Angel/Pilgrim

This is the Cathedral door which if it was open would let you into the cloister – but it is usually shut tight. It has two names.

Angel comes from a depiction of the archangel Michael which used to be on an altarpiece in the cloister.

Pilgrim refers to the pilgrims who would enter the cathedral by this door. Spot the scallop shell which you can see above the door. The scallop shell is used as a marker of the Saint James Way followed by pilgrims to Santiago de Compostela.

The door itself is covered in little gothic flowers.

Above the door you can see an intricate carving of lauburus.

The lauburu, sometimes called the Basque cross, is a traditional Basque Country symbol which is said to represent the culture and identify of the region.

Map 12.5 – Face the door and turn right to reach a crossroads.

Map 12.6 - Turn left into Calle La Torre and walk along to the next corner on the left.

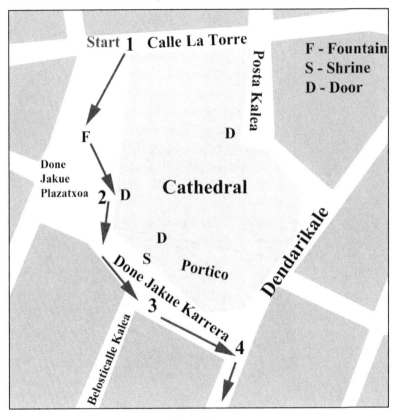

Map 13

Map 13.1 - Take the next left to reach Done Jakue Plazatoa.

Done Jakue Plazatoa

This pretty square has a fountain, and on one side you will find Santiago Cathedral.

Santiago Cathedral

There has been a religious building on this site from the time Bilbao was just a small fishing village. Originally it was a small church with a cemetery. It was replaced by a larger church which only lasted a very short time as it burned in a fire.

Pope Gregory XI financed a third church by granting indulgences for alms. An indulgence is, according to the Catholic Church:

> "A way to reduce the amount of punishment
> one has to undergo for sins".

So in other words, those who could afford it paid to get off lightly for their sins, and in the process Bilbao got its new church.

It was built in the gothic style and was started in the fourteenth century, completed in the sixteenth century, and only declared a cathedral in 1950.

It was badly damaged in the floods of 1983 and Bilbao began a massive restoration project to save it. In 2000 it was completed and today you can see it restored to perfect condition.

It is named after Saint James because Bilbao sits on the Way of Saint James.

Bilbao's football team's stadium has a nickname of La Catedral, but that nickname was used long before this church became a cathedral. The team's logo does have a church on it, but it's not this one.

The Exterior

The huge main door is guarded by Saint Peter and Saint Paul – Peter is the one holding the keys.

The Tower

The tower you see now is the fourth version. The previous tower was demolished at the start of the nineteenth century, and this one was finished in 1883.

The top of the tower was built in a lighter coloured stone which was brought from France. It holds eleven bells.

Inside the Cathedral

If it's open go inside and explore. Your ticket includes a useful audio guide. It also gives you entry to the Saint Anton church which you will visit later.

First enjoy the white ribbed ceiling and the beautiful stained glass windows which surround you as you walk down the nave. You can see the unusual corridor which runs around the perimeter on the upper floor.

Downstairs the Cathedral has many chapels, and the audio guide will point you to the most interesting things to see.

The Crypt

Don't miss descending to the crypt, where you can see the remains of the first little hermitage which the Cathedral stands on.

The Cloister

The cloister is beautifully constructed with columns and arches. In the middle is a little garden with lush trees.

Find the tomb of Francisco Iturribarría which is a relatively recent addition – 1957. He is being watched over by two beautiful angels.

Cathedral Portico

As you walk down Done Jakue Karrera, you will find on your left, the huge arched portico of the cathedral.

Once built, it became the place where the earliest town councils could take shelter from the Basque weather when needed, as they used to meet in the open air. However the portico was really built to hold the cathedral up!

The land the cathedral stands on was marshy and subsidence was always a problem. So the portico was built on this side as a buttress, to effectively prop the cathedral up.

The Portico Door

At the back of the portico is the cathedral's third great door.

Above the door is the city's coat of arms, and beneath it you will see a series of intricately carved arches. The outermost one is decorated with fourteen seated prophets.

The Shrine of Belosticalle Kalea

Spot the little shrine attached to one of the outer pillars of the portico. It's at the end of Belosticalle Kalea.

The Seven Streets each had a little shrine like this one which honoured the street's patron saint. Each street held a festival on its saint's day, but sadly that custom has more or less died out.

The Mary Magdalene statue in the shrine isn't the original as it got pinched in the twentieth century. Its replacement was placed behind glass to ensure it stayed put.

If you happen to be here on June 22nd which is the feast day of Mary Magdalene, you will find flowers placed below the shrine.

Map 13.3 - Continue down Done Jakue Karrera. You will reach a T-junction with Dendarikale.

Map 13.4 - Turn right along Dendarikale.

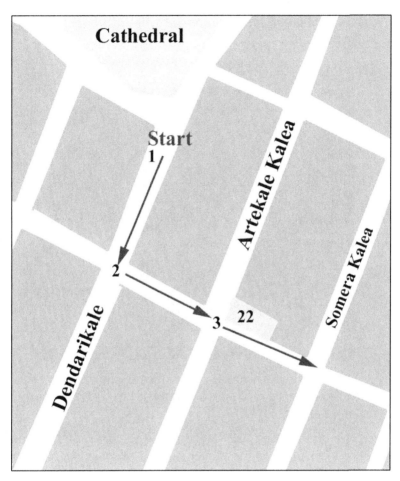

Map 13

Map 13.1 – Walk along Dendarikale to reach the next narrow street on the left, Canton Julián Echevarría Camarón.

Map 13,2 – Turn left into Canton Julián Echevarría Camarón and you will reach a crossroads with Artekale Kalea.

81

On the left-hand corner opposite you, at number 22, is a much loved fish shop.

Salted Cod

Salted Cod is a favourite dish of the Spanish, and this is Bilbao's oldest, most famous, and most loved shop. There is usually a queue!

The owner, Gregorio Martin, put the shop-sign in the shape of a cod up on the corner in 1930. It reads:

> Gregorio Martín.
> Specialty in soaked cod every day.
> Tno.- 13,707"

Have a look in the window, or even venture in to have a look around.

The reason cod is so popular in Bilbao and why there are so many ways of cooking it, is down to a fishmonger called Gurtubay.

The story goes that in 1835 he sent an order for "100 or 120" cod to his supplier. However his handwritten note was misread as 1,000,120 cod. When his order arrived he had no choice but to sell it in any guise he could.

It was actually a blessing in disguise as Bilbao was starving, because the city was under siege due to the Carlist Wars. The people were more than thankful to have cod every day, cooked in every possible way. So Gurtubay became very rich instead of going bust!

Map 13.3 – Facing the shop, go down its right-hand side along Canton Julián Echevarría Camarón to reach Somera Kalea.

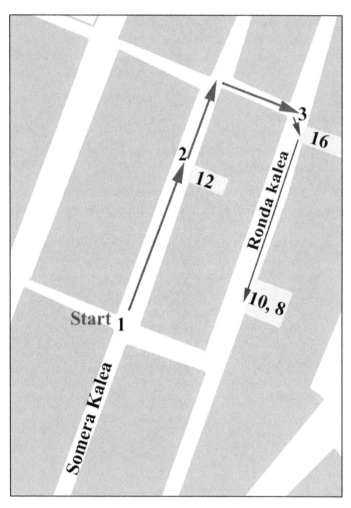

Map 14

Map 14.1 - Turn left and walk down Somera Kalea to reach a wooden door at number 12 on your right.

The Spanish Mozart

At the end of this walk you will see the Teatro Arriaga – an impressive building by anyone's standards. It was dedicated to composer Juan Crisóstomo de Arriaga who was born and lived as a child at number 12. You can see a plaque commemorating him. There is also a carved head above the door which presumably also commemorates him

Arriaga was called the "Spanish Mozart". Both composers were born on January 27th, but fifty years apart. Like Mozart, Arriaga was a child prodigy and composed an opera aged just 13. Sadly also like Mozart he died very young, at 19 from tuberculosis. He was buried in an unmarked grave in Montmartre in Paris, just as Mozart lies in an unmarked grave in Vienna.

Map 14.2 - Continue down Somera Kalea and take the first on your right. It's a very narrow street which will take you onto Calle Ronda.

Calle Ronda

This is not actually one of the original seven streets - it was where the town wall ran. The current street name, Ronda, comes from the fact that the town guards walked around the city wall and this was part of their route. As the town expanded the wall was replaced by more houses, but the street name stuck.

Map 14.3 – Opposite you is number 16. Take a few steps to the right along Calle Ronda to reach a plaque.

Miguel Unamuno Again

It was in this street that Miguel Unamuno was born and lived as a child, and there is a plaque here to commemorate his arrival.

Map 14.4 – Continue along Calle Ronda to reach numbers 10 and 8.

Section of old Town Wall

As mentioned, parts of the old town wall have been incorporated into those buildings which replaced the wall when Bilbao expanded. Here you can see the original old stone wall.

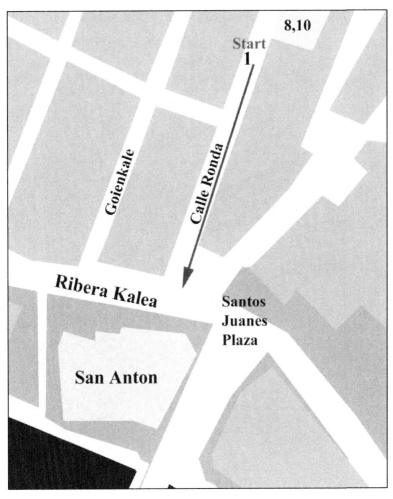

Start

1

Goienkale

Calle Ronda

Ribera Kalea

Santos
Juanes
Plaza

San Anton

Map 15

Map 15.1 – Keep walking along Calle Ronda and you will exit the Seven Streets onto Ribera Kalea, near the river.

On the opposite side of Ribera Kalea stands the church of San Anton.

Map 16

Map 16.1 - Cross busy Ribera Kalea using the nearby zebra crossing. It will take you to the corner of the San Anton church.

Map 16.2 – Use the second zebra crossing to get to the left-hand side of the bridge. Then turn right to walk straight ahead and onto the San Anton Bridge.

Take a look at the second building on the opposite shore.

Casa Cuna (Cradle House)

You will see the pretty Casa Cuna. It's very decorative Modernist façade doesn't face the river but you will see it soon.

Map 16.3 - Walk to the midway point across the bridge.

The San Anton Bridge

The bridge you are standing on is the oldest in the city and was first built in 1318. Both it and the church appear on Bilbao's coat of arms.

The two wolves on the coat of arms refer to Don Diego Lopez who turned Bilbao into a town – the name Lopez means Wolves.

When the San Anton Bridge was built, it was the only one crossing the river, meaning merchants and traders travelled to this point to cross the river. This was all good for Bilbao's trade and importance. In fact the Bilboans went to great lengths to make sure their bridge stayed the only river crossing for a long time!

The bridge was also the site of execution of nobles in medieval times; the executioner simply tied a stone to the victim's neck and threw him in! Mere commoners where usually sent to the gallows.

The bridge has been damaged, knocked down, and rebuilt many times over the centuries.

Turn round to look back at the church - This is the best viewpoint.

The Tower

The church tower was added in the eighteenth century and it is classed as Baroque – which means it is intricately decorated.

Look right to the top to see the Giraldillo – an eight foot bronze female statue which is said to celebrate the victory of Christianity over the Muslim faith in Spain.

Map 16.4 – Turn away from the church and continue over the bridge.

Take the first left along Urazurrutia Kalea. The Casa Cuna is the second building on the left.

Casa Cuna Facade

The Casa Cuna was founded from public funds in 1912. It provided a nursery for the children of the poor who must work but who have no other means of childcare.

It has been beautifully restored and is still a public services building.

There is a lovely statue of the Virgin Mary and the Baby Jesus above the door – which is very appropriate for a nursery.

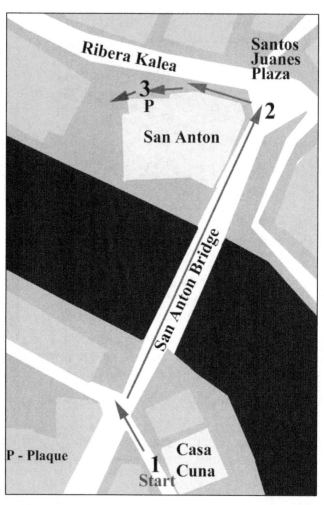

Map 17

Map 17.1 – Backtrack to the corner. Turn right to return across the bridge to Ribera Kalea.

Map 17.2 - Turn left to walk alongside the church. Pause when you reach an engraved memorial on the church wall.

Estanco de la Sal Rebellion Plaque

This plaque was put up in memory of six men executed in Bilbao in 1634.

The Spanish Crown was strapped for cash because of its endless wars in Northern Europe and it took drastic action. It requisitioned the area of Biscay's salt reserves and bumped the price up by 44%. Since salt was vital to preserve food the cost of food rocketed in consequence.

In the Basque region the people rebelled, and two thousand men gathered in Guernica to demand the removal of the new tax laws. The rebellion included demonstrations, uprisings, and one assassination

The leaders of the rebellion were eventually captured. As might have been expected they were executed, but King Philip decided that enough was enough, No further arrests were made and the taxes were abolished.

The result was that an uneasy peace returned between the Basque people and the Spanish crown.

Map 17.3 – Continue to the corner of the church where you will find the main entrance.

San Anton Church

Merchant caravans arriving into Bilbao from Castile used a nearby ford to cross the river safely. A fortress was built near the fort to protect the caravans and their cargo.

Don Diego Lopez read out Bilbao's founding charter near the fortress, and the settlement of Bilbao became a town. The area around the fortress was later swept up by Bilbao and the town wall was extended around it.

San Anton church was completed in the fifteenth century and stands where the fortress once stood.

It is this church which is on the logo of Athletic Bilbao football club.

The Porch and Balcony

To be honest it's an odd looking church from this side.

The church was originally built in the Gothic style. However the porch and balcony which you can see on the corner were given rounded arches rather than pointed ones and so are classified as Renaissance.

The balcony above the main entrance seems very out-of-place. Even odder, the door which gives access to the balcony can only be reached from the church by crossing the roof!

The reason is that the balcony was never really used by the church. Town Council offices which are now long gone, were built right next door to the church, and the balcony could be reached directly from there.

So it was used by town officials when something interesting was going on in the Plaza Vieja (Old Square) which the balcony overlooked – a parade perhaps or a public execution.

The Door

There is an engraving above the door which declares the importance of the church:

Agregada a la Basílica de San Juan de Letrán

Attached to the Basilica of Saint John Lateran

The Basilica of Saint John Lateran is Rome's cathedral and its bishop is The Pope.

Go inside.

The Church

When you walk inside the church itself, you can see evidence of the church's original Gothic design all around you; a ribbed vaulted ceiling, pointed arches, and stained glass windows. This church also has an upper corridor running around the perimeter, just like the one in the Cathedral.

At one time burials took place inside the church. When it was restructured the tomb markers were used in part to reconstruct the church floor. The remains of the cemetery residents were saved and placed in the ossuary which is downstairs.

Secret passages

Find the St Lucia chapel. There is a door on one side which leads to some stairs which have been bricked up.

The popular theory is that it gave access to the next-door Council Offices. That would let the officials enter the church while bypassing any citizens who might have a complaint for them to deal with. Nobody really knows.

Ancient Foundations

Near the altar is a glass floor which lets you see down to the foundations of a very ancient tower which once stood there. The Town Wall was extended to envelop the church. So also near the altar you can see some remnants of the wall.

Don Klaudio Gallastegui

There is a bust of Don Klaudio Gallastegui in the church. He became the priest of San Anton in 1938. At that time the area around the church was poverty stricken and his congregation was very small. He soon changed that as people flocked to hear him preach.

He raised his voice against the poverty of the people, and he was called:

La voz de los sin voz

or

The voice of the voiceless

as it says on the plaque below the bust.

He also raised his voice loudly against Franco which brought him both a lot of problems but also the adulation of his congregation.

He conducted the first mass in Basque in Bilbao. Bilbao named a street after him.

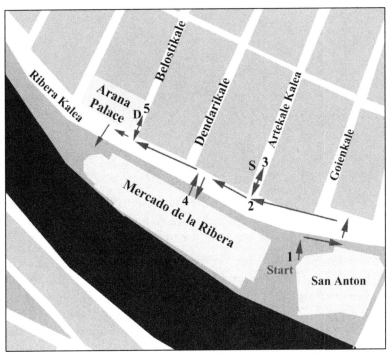

Map 18

Map 18.1 - When you have seen enough of the church, exit and turn right to find the nearest zebra crossing. Use it to cross Ribera Kalea.

Once over turn left. Pass Goienkale on your right.

Map 18.2 – Take the next right into Artekale Kalea, but just a few steps.

97

La Santísima Trinidad

On your left you will see La Santísima Trinidad in a niche behind glass. This is Artekale Kalea's shrine which honours the Holy Trinity. It has always had a lamp above it.

Doña Dionisia lived next to the shrine, and she took it upon herself to feed the lamp and keep the light shining. However she died during a smallpox epidemic and no-one else took on the job, so the shrine fell into darkness. Her brother was a song-writer and wrote about his sister and the flame of the shrine. You can hear it here:

https://www.youtube.com/watch?v=oh9DosiWugU&t=19s

These days the lamp is electric, so the shrine is always lit up at night.

Map 18.3 – Backtrack to return to Ribera Kalea. Turn right to reach another handy zebra crossing.

Mercado de la Ribera

You will see the central door of the enormous art deco Mercado de La Ribera on the other side of the street.

It stands on what was the Plaza Vieja until the start of the nineteenth century. That was when the city developers decided that the Old Square could be put to better use and built on top of it.

The market has a plaque proclaiming it's the biggest in Europe, and even if that's not completely true these days, it's certainly huge.

It has gorgeous stained glass windows letting the light stream in.

It was built to provide traders with a ventilated and hygienic market place rather than market stalls in the sun, and it's renowned for its ultra-fresh fish and food of all types. The market has undergone extensive restoration and is worth a look inside and a browse around.

Cross Ribera Kalea and go in to explore - you might consider it as a stop for coffee or lunch.

Exit by the same door as you entered by!

Map 18.4 – When you exit the market you should be facing Ribera Kalea.

Cross Ribera Kalea once more and turn left to walk along the arcade.

Pass Dendarikale on your right, then pause at the corner of the next street on your right, Belostikale.

The building on the corner in front of you is the Arana Palace. Take a few steps into Belostikale.

Arana Palace

You will find the main door of what's thought to be the oldest palace in Bilbao on your left. It dates from the late sixteenth century.

Its handsome main door is decorated with two figures said to be Hercules – he's probably about to murder some mythical beast with his hammer.

Map 18.5 – Backtrack to Ribera Kalea.

Turn right along the arcade which runs along the front of the Palace.

Use the first nearby zebra crossing to get over Ribera Kalea.

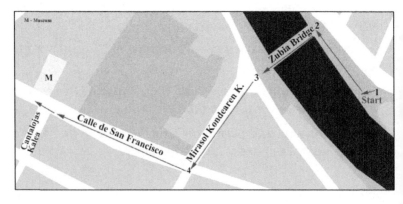

Map 19

Map 19.1 – Once over turn right to reach the Ribera Zubia footbridge.

Zubia Bridge

This was the only footbridge over the river until the Zubi Zuri footbridge was constructed. You may already have crossed the Zubi Zuri on walk 1.

Pedestrians at one time were charged a toll to cross it, but it is now free.

You now have another choice to make:

Reproductions Museum

Bilbao has an interesting museum just a five minute walk away on the other side of the river. It is the Reproductions Museum and as its title hints, it holds reproductions of some of the world's greatest sculptures and buildings. It was built to help students study the world's great pieces.

If you enjoy looking at ancient sculptures you will probably appreciate it. However if that museum doesn't appeal, continue from "Back into the Old Town" on page 103.

Otherwise, to reach the Reproductions Museum:

Map 19.2 – Cross the river via the Ribera Zubia footbridge.

Map 19.3 - Go up Mirasol Kondearen Kalea which is directly in front of you.

Map 19.4 Take the first right, Calle de San Francisco, and continue along it until you pass Calle Cantalojas on your left.

The museum is on your right just a few steps further.

Museo de Reproducciones Artísticas

Inside you will find reproductions of many of the greatest sculptures to be found. See Michelangelo's Moses without visiting Rome, or the Pergamum Altar without visiting Berlin.

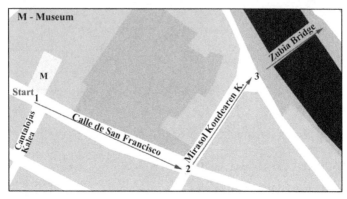

Map 20

Map 20.1 - Once you have had enough, exit the museum and turn left to walk along Calle de San Francisco.

Map 20.2 - Take the first left to go downhill towards the river once more.

Map 20.3 - Re-cross the Ribera Zubia footbridge.

Back into the Old Town

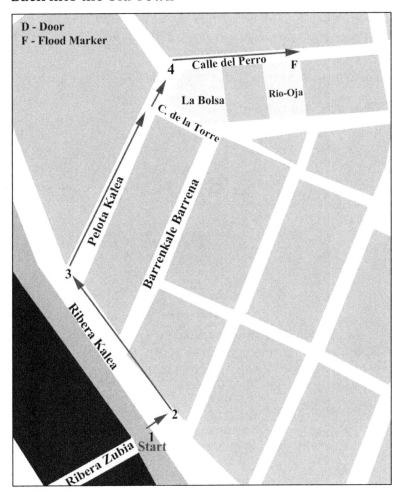

Map 21

Map 21.1 – With the bridge behind you cross Ribera Kalea.

Map 21.2 – Turn left and walk along Ribera Kalea to reach the second street on the right, Pelota Kalea.

Map 21.3 – Turn right into Pelota Kalea. Pass little Calle de la Torre on your right.

Pause just before the corner of Andra Maria Kalea which is the next street on your left.

Spot the little statue of the Virgin on the left-hand wall.

Change from the Pot

As in many cities, the working men of Bilbao would often go for a drink at the end of the week. Part of the evening's routine was each drinker putting money into a "pot" to buy the rounds.

Here you see a little likeness of the Virgin and a collection box beneath her. It's rather unusual in that the Virgin is holding a wine glass in her right hand.

Tradition says that any change from the "pot" should be deposited with the Virgin. On her celebration day, the money donated by everyone is extracted and given to charities. So if you are passing after a pleasant night out, you could drop a coin or two in.

This seems an excellent tradition to me, and it should be adopted by other cities!

Opposite the Virgin is an interesting building which has two nicknames; La Bolsa and Yhon's Palace.

La Bolsa/Yhon's Palace

The first building on this spot was a tower house and the home of one of Bilbao's powerful families in the fourteenth century. Through the generations the original building was expanded and beautified and remained a family home.

That changed in the eighteenth century when the owner rented the ground floor to some merchants from Eastern Europe, and they opened a hardware store. One of their employees was Leandro Yhon who soon became the head of the business. He made the store a "palace" where everyone came to buy luxury goods, which explains one of the building's nicknames.

It's also thought that merchants make deals and trades here – hence its other nickname "La Bolsa"

Another urban story tells us that the "Palace" had a "smuggler's" passage which ran into the nearby river – perhaps it did and that is where some of the luxury goods came from.

Exterior

The main door has a really unusual carved lintel running around it. Above the door is a statue of the Virgin of Begoña. It replaces the Palace's original statue which was thrown into the river during the 1917 General Strike.

Interior

The palace interior is definitely worth visiting if it's open. It has a beautiful courtyard and stairway. You can also see part of the original old tower-house where this building began. So if it's open you might want to pop in.

Map 21.4 – Stand facing the door of La Bolsa. Turn left to go along Calle del Perro.

Pause at number 4 on your right-hand side. Take a few steps further along the street to find the main entrance – at the time of writing it is a restaurant.

Flood Marker

Here you will find another 1983 flood marker. The red line at the top of the marker shows how high the waters reached.

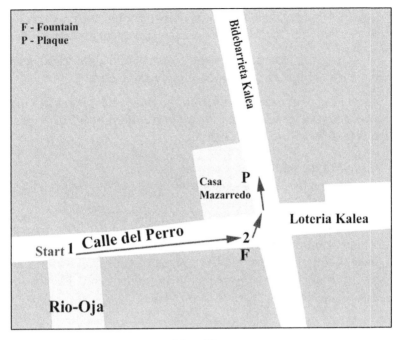

Map 22

Map 22.1 – Continue along Calle del Perro to the next crossroads.

Fuente Del Perro

On your right you will find a very old fountain. It is called the Fountain of the Dog, even though the three animal heads you see are actually lions.

Local legend tells us that the locals had never seen a lion, so they just assumed that the animals on the fountain were dogs.

It seems unlikely that no-one in Bilbao had ever seen a picture of a lion. However it must be said that the lion heads don't look like a traditional lion – their appearance was inspired by stylized Egyptian lions. So perhaps we really can't blame the locals for not recognising them as such.

At the top you can see the construction date 1800, and beneath the lions is a stone Roman sarcophagus.

Map 22.2 - Facing the fountain, go down the street behind you, Bidebarrieta Kalea. Pause at number 14 which is just a few steps along on your left.

Casa Mazarredo
This relatively modern blue and white building is the Casa Mazarredo.

It was built on the foundations of a much older palace, where Admiral Mazarredo was born in 1793. He is said to have been the most skilled Spanish sailor, navigator and tactician of the time. As a memorial to his name, his coat of arms has been placed on the first floor.

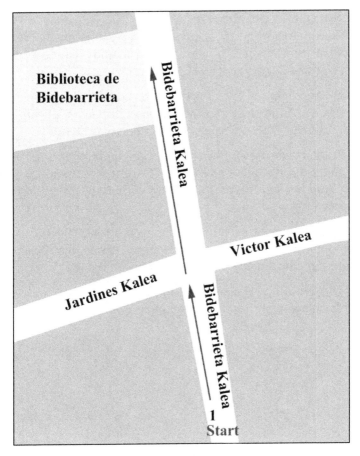

Map 23

Map 23.1 - Continue along this street crossing a junction with Victor Kalea and Jardines Kalea.

A few more steps will bring you to the Biblioteca de Bidebarrieta on your left.

Biblioteca de Bidebarrieta

This historic library is open to the public and is really worth a look around. Inside you will find beautiful halls, stairways, and reading rooms.

It was originally built for the Historic and Liberal Society, in honour of the men who held Bilbao in a siege during the Carlist Wars. The society's original name was El Sitio.

Franco ordered appropriation of the building in 1937 – he probably did not want any Liberal Societies in Spain! It was later sold back to Bilbao, and Bilbao turned it into the library you see now.

If you manage to see inside the auditorium, face the stage and look up to the right. You will see a mannequin of Miguel Unamuno who sits in splendid isolation on the first floor.

The building is also used for musical events and it is worth checking if there is one on during your visit.

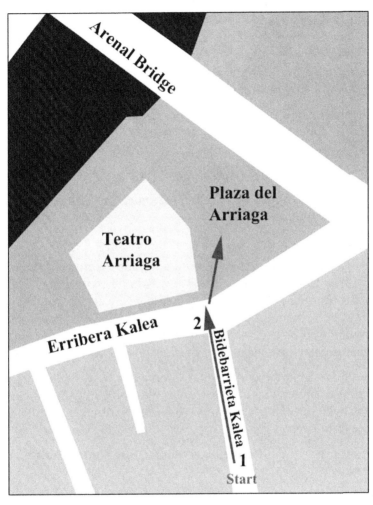

Map 24

Map 24.1 – Exit the library. With the library behind you, turn left to continue down Bidebarrieta Kalea.

Map 24.2 - Cross Erribera Kalea to reach Plaza del Arriaga.

Plaza del Arriaga

The Semana Grande is a manic 9 day festival held every year in August and is centred here. The fair was started quite recently in 1978, as the city shook off the strictures and rules of the Franco era, and started to come alive again.

There are dances, sports, food stalls, music, competitions, and of course fireworks all day and most of the night. You can have a look via this link

https://www.youtube.com/watch?v=rh9N1CNtWYM

The ornate building which overlooks the square is the Teatro Arriaga.

Teatro Arriaga

The current theatre replaced an older theatre which was built in 1890. The older theatre was built using state of the art technology of the time. Its audiences were as impressed by the electric lighting as the show, and the Bilbaons were so enamoured by their theatre that they could even phone in to hear the performance. That theatre burned down in 1914.

It was rebuilt just five years later, and was designed by the same architect who built the Town Hall – if you tackle Walk 1 you will see the similarities. He was inspired by the Paris Opera house.

The theatre offers guided tours. Check this website for details

https://www.teatroarriaga.eus/quienes-somos/visitas-guiadas/?lang=en

The Spanish Mozart

This theatre is dedicated to Juan Crisóstomo de Arriaga, the "Spanish Mozart", who you read about earlier.

The theatre has had good times and bad times. It was shut during the Spanish Civil war, reopened and flourished, only to fall into total disrepair in the seventies and eighties. It was badly damaged by the 1983 floods but was rebuilt two years later in its present lovely form.

You have now reached the end of this walk.

Walk 3 - Arenal Bridge to the Museum of Fine Arts

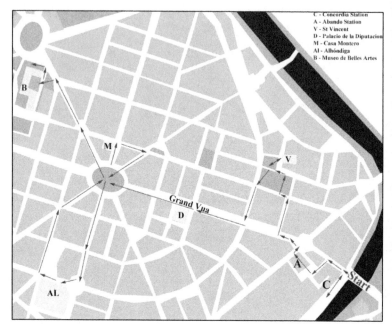

Walk 3 Overview

This walk will take you from the Arenal Bridge at the edge of the old town, through the Ensanche, finishing at the Museum of Fine Arts

The Ensanche is the name given to the expansion area across the river from the old town. It was where people and businesses with money and ambition moved to and built to impress.

The walk ends at Bilbao's second major art museum - classical art this time.

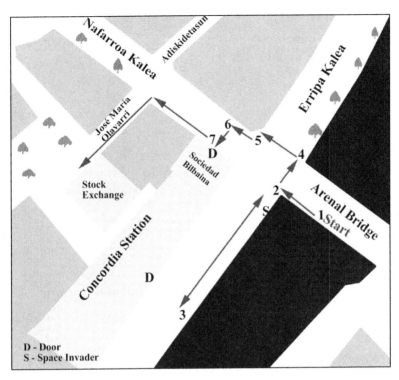

Map 1

This walk starts half-way across the Arenal Bridge.

From the Bridge

Look upstream and towards the right-hand river-bank. Spot the Concordia Station with its gorgeous green and yellow Belle Époque façade.

Space Invaders

If you are old enough to remember space invaders from the eighties, you might like to spot one of Bilbao's.

At the time of writing there is one attached to the side of the embankment. It's near the Arenal Bridge and on the same side of the river as the Concordia Station. You can spot it from the bridge.

There are several sprinkled around European cities. They were put there by someone who is thought to be French and who calls himself The Invader.

Map 1.1 – Turn right and walk to the end of the bridge.

You are now in Abando which was a separate town until it was annexed by Bilbao in 1876.

Map 1.2 – Turn left and climb the steps to reach the front of Concordia station.

Concordia Station

Now you can get a close look at the lovely floral decorations which run across the top of the windows. Above the entrance just beneath the clock it declares

F C de Santander a Bilbao

The station opened in 1902 and provided a rail link between Bilbao and Santander – the ancient port which lies about 75 kilometres along the coast.

Turn round to get a very good view of the Old Town. There are some handy benches if you want a sit-down.

Map 1.3 – Return down the steps to the bridge. Use the zebra crossing in front of you to cross to the other side of the bridge.

Map 1.4 - Turn left and use another zebra crossing to cross Erripa Kalea.

Map 1.5 - Now walk straight ahead along Calle Navarra. Pause after a few steps and look across the road to have a look at the Sociedad Bilbaina building.

Sociedad Bilbaina

This is home to one of the most prestigious private clubs in Bilbao.

The club started life In Plaza Neuva, which you may have already seen on walk 2, but it moved in 1939 to this much grander home.

It has beautiful club rooms, games rooms, and a huge important library. Unbelievably in this day and age, it still bars women from being members.

The restaurant and the English Bar are open to the public which might tempt you for a drink or a meal later.

Map 1.6 –Carefully cross Calle Navarra to reach the columned door of the Sociedad Bilbaina.

Map 1.7 - Turn right and walk along Calle Navarra. Take the next left, José María Olavarri Kalea.

You will walk into a square where you will find the elegant Stock Exchange Building on your left. It has BOLSA written over the door.

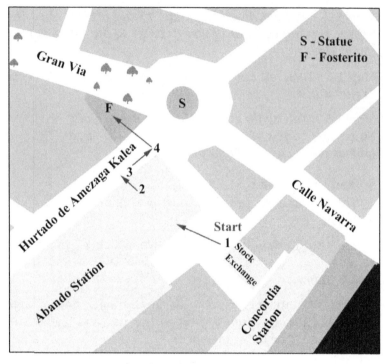

Map 2

Opposite the Stock Exchange stands Abando Station.

Map 2.1 - Climb the steps to find the station entrance. Go into the station – please note which door you enter by.

Abando Station

It's a much bigger and grander station than Concorida, as it should be as it's the main entry point into Bilbao by train.

The station is actually on the second floor, so climb the stairs to reach it.

It is huge and built in riveted steel, and it has a massive beautiful stained glass window which is worth seeing. It depicts Bilboan working life in the industrial age.

The central clock is surrounded by mountains and above it is the Basilica de Begoña. Around that you can see steelworkers, bridges, farmers, and other figures and landmarks from life around Bilbao.

Indalecio Prieto

You will find a large and rather odd bust of Indalecio Prieto on the upper concourse.

So who was Indalecio Prieto? He was a socialist politician from Bilbao. After many years in and out of favour with the Spanish government, he fled to Mexico when Franco took over, never to return. He led the Socialist Party in Exile from Mexico until he died there in 1962.

Name Change

To honour him, this station's official name was changed from Abando to Abando Indalecio Prieto in 2006. The Bibloans were furious that their station had been renamed by Madrid, with no consultation with Bilbao on the matter. So despite the new boards all over the station using the full name, to the locals it is still Abando Station.

Return to the ground floor when you are ready to move on.

Map 2.2 - Exit by the door directly opposite the one you entered by. This will take you to Hurtado de Amezaga Kalea.

Map 2.3 – Turn right to reach a busy plaza. Pause at the corner of Hurtado de Amezaga Kalea to take a look above the door on your right-hand side.

Franco Era

The plaza was renamed during Franco's rule to Plaza de Espana, and you can see one of the old street-signs from that time here. It was of course a ploy to remind the Basques who was in charge. It was renamed to Plaza Biribila in 1995.

Don Diego López de Haro

In the middle you can see Don Diego López de Haro. He holds the charter which bestowed city rights to Bilbao in his hand. Each year on the anniversary of the city's founding there is a civic procession to the statue where a wreath is laid.

The statue started life in Plaza Nueva, was moved here, then back to Plaza Nueva, and finally back here. Let's hope he stays this time.

Map 2.4 – Use the zebra crossing to cross Hurtado de Amezaga Kalea.

Walk straight ahead and along Calle Gran Vía Diego López de Haro, which is commonly called Gran Via. It is the main thoroughfare of Bilbao.

Norman Foster

You will pass one of the Fosteritos, an entrance into the modern metro system. The name is an affectionate tribute to Norman Foster who designed them.

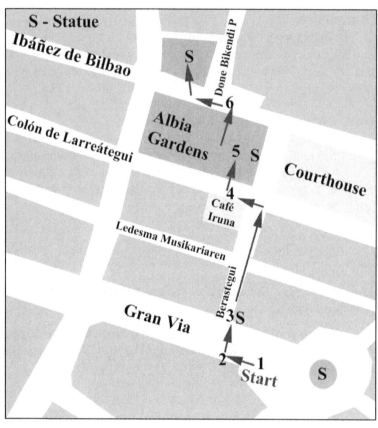

Map 3

Map 3.1– Continue to walk along the Grand Via and you will reach another zebra crossing.

Map 3.2 - Use it to Cross Grand Via. You will see Calle Berastegui in front of you.

Look up to the corner between Gran Via and Calle Berastegui to see a statue of the goddess Athena.

Map 3.3 - Walk straight ahead along pedestrianized Calle Berastegui. Cross the junction with Ledesma Musikariaren Kalea

Keep walking, and you will reach a crossroads with Colón de Larreátegui Kalea. Turn left to cross Calle Berastegui and you will find Café Iruna at the corner.

Café Iruna

This is a lovely art deco Café, worth going into even if all you want is a coffee.

Sit down and look around. It has a number of different sitting spaces and is decorated with tiles and Mudejar decoration – inspired by the Moors from North Africa.

It was much loved by Bilbao's writing class; including Unamuno whose square you visited on Walk 2.

Map 3.4 - When you are ready to move on, cross Colón de Larreátegui Kaleaand and walk into the Albia Gardens.

You will see three paths in front of you; take the middle path to reach a statue.

Albia Gardens

This little park is much loved by the locals. This was originally the centre of the village of Abando before it was gobbled up by Bilbao in the nineteenth century.

There are actually two gardens and the one you are in now is the larger one.

Sabino Arano

Sabino was born in Abando not long after it had been annexed by Bilbao.

He became professor of the Basque language, and fought for its survival as Spain made Spanish the mandatory language to be used in schools and cultural events. He formulated a standard Basque grammar as part of his battle to save the language.

Politically he wanted independence for Biscay and wrote many articles giving reasons and justifications for independence.

Some of his ideas were less admirable than others. He believed in the purity of the Basque people and its moral supremacy over others. He was also against Spanish immigration into the Basque country

He founded the Basque Nationalist Party and is thought by many to be the father of Basque Nationalism.

He even thought up the name for the Basque countries, and on his statue you can read:

Euzkotarren aberria Euzkadi da

Euzkadi is the country of the Basques.

Map 4.5 – Facing the statue, turn left to exit the park onto Ibáñez de Bilbao Kalea.

Map 4.6 – Cross Ibáñez de Bilbao Kalea and turn left. Take the next right into Done Bikendi Plaza where you will see the smaller of the Albia Gardens.

Walk into it and you will find a statue of the Virgin Mary surrounded by a railing.

Virgin Mary

When this statue was first installed, the people were shocked because her gown seemed far too revealing. So this version, with abundant flowing robes, quickly took its place.

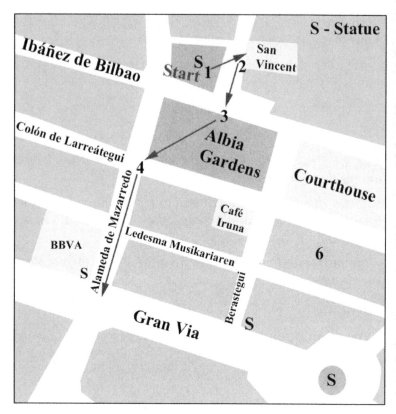

Map 5

Map 5.1 - Standing face to face with the statue, you will see the San Vincent de Abando church behind her. If it's open pop in, as it's beautiful inside.

San Vincent de Abando

The first church which stood here, like many other churches of the time, placed the tombs of its congregation inside. Eventually it was so full of tombs that a new church was needed.

This Renaissance church was built in the sixteenth century. The huge triumphal arch over the entrance is

126

similar to the one you might have seen if you visited the Basilica de Begoña on Walk 2.

Inside you will find tall Doric columns and another beautiful ribbed ceiling.

Explore the various chapels to see the five golden altarpieces.

Make sure you take a look at the very modern work "The Last Supper" by Basque artist Ignacio García-Ergüin. Usually The Last Supper is painted looking along the table horizontally, rather than this unusual angle. It's very effective.

Map 5.2 - When you exit the church turn left to return to Ibáñez de Bilbao Kalea.

Map 5.3 - Cross the Albia gardens diagonally right to reach the junction of Colón de Larreátegui Kalea and Alameda de Mazarredo.

Map 5.4 – Walk down Alameda de Mazarredo away from the park. Cross the junction with Ledesma Musikariaren and continue straight ahead to reach the Gran Via once more.

Stand at the corner to see the BBVA building on your right at its best.

Mercury

The door is guarded by two lions, and a line of columns marches along the building on both sides.

Look right to the top to see Mercury high above you pointing to the stars. He is the god of financial gain amongst other things, so very suitable for a huge bank.

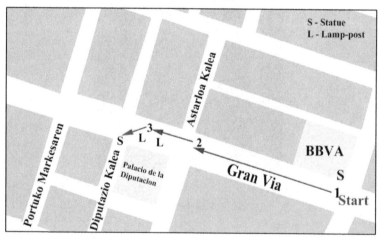

Map 6

Map 6.1 – With Mercury and the BBVA building on your right, walk straight ahead on Gran Via to the next crossroads.

Map 6.2 – Cross Astarloa Kalea and you will see the Palacio de la Diputacion on your left.

Palacio de la Diputacion (Palace of the Council)

This impressive building is the seat of provincial Government. The government used to govern from a building in Plaza Nueva, but more space was needed so a new building was planned and this is the result

It front of the palace are two splendid lampposts, topped by eagles that are holding the lamps in their beaks.

The Palace bears the Bilbao coat of arms in the middle of the ornate façade.

Inside is just as decorative as outside with stained glass windows and a striking staircase. You can tour the building but you have to pre-book your places.

Map 6.3 – Continue along Gran Via, but just as far as the next street on the left, Diputazio Kalea. Here you will find a bust of John Adams

John Adams

He was the second president of the USA and he visited Bilbao in 1780, not long after the American War of Independence.

The plaque beneath the bust displays an extract from one of his letters, and it tells us why he came.

> This extraordinary people have preserved their ancient language, genius, laws, government and manners, without innovation, longer than any other nation in Europe".

It's said that what he found here had an impact on the constitution of the USA; it was being written in the same year as his visit.

Any country would appreciate such a glowing statement so it's not surprising that Bilbao decided to erect a statue to make sure people knew about it. The bust was created in 2009.

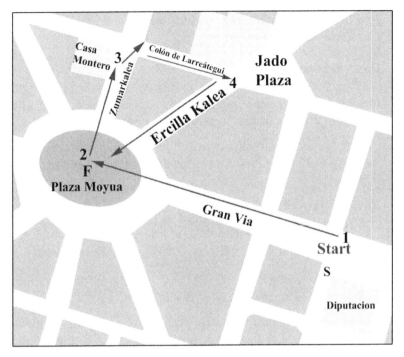

Map 7

Map 7.1 - Continue along Gran Via and you will reach Plaza Moyua. You will see a fosterito on both your left and right.

Cross to the middle of the square to have a look around.

Plaza Moyua

This roundabout is decorated with a lovely fountain and colourful gardens, and you could sit on one of the benches running around it for a rest.

Map 7.2 – Stand with the Via Grand behind you.

Turn right to leave the square on Alameda Recalde Zumarkalea.

Just before you reach the next crossroads, and on your left at number 34, is Montero House.

Casa Montero

This 1902 building is very ornate with flowing lines and few sharp corners; the balconies are especially beautiful. The door is just as decorative with curling ironwork on the glass.

The locals have nicknamed it Gaudi's House. Not because he designed it or stayed there, but just because it is definitely in his style.

Gaudi is quoted as saying:

> There are no straight lines or sharp corners in nature,
> Therefore, buildings must have no straight lines or sharp corners.

It looks like the architect of this building, agreed with him.

The cited architect was Marcelino Luis de Aladrén Mendívil. He also designed the Palacio de la Diputación in Gran Via which you saw not long ago. The two buildings are worlds apart in style, and you would never think they were the work of the same person.

Well they weren't really. Aladrén Mendívil died in 1902 and this building was completed in 1903 by Jean Batiste Darroguy who was part of the Aladrén studio. It's said he redesigned the façade to suit his own artistic leanings.

Map 7.3 – Continue to the crossroads and then turn right into Colón de Larreátegui Kalea. Walk to the end of the street to reach triangular Jado Plaza.

Jado Plaza

As you do, you will see another of Bilbao's most eye-catching apartment buildings on your left. It's covered in sculpture and iron or stone balconies. The corner of the building is especially good – who wouldn't want to stand on that top balcony.

In the middle of the plaza is another pretty fountain, decorated with stone lions.

Map 7.4 – Return to the corner of Colón de Larreátegui Kalea - it is the street you entered the plaza by.

Turn left to walk to walk down Ercilla Kalea. This will take you back to Plaza Moyua.

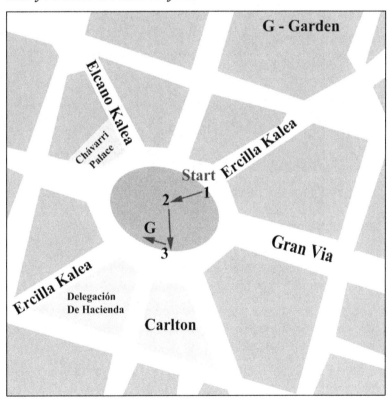

Map 8

Map 8.1 – Walk into the centre of the square.

Orientate yourself by turning right to find the oldest-looking building on the square. That is the Chávarri Palace. Walk towards it to get a better look.

Chávarri Palace

It is where the Biscay Civil Government sits. Its design is very unusual. firstly because of its Flemish style, and secondly because of its windows.

It's Flemish because the businessman who commissioned it, Victor Chávarri, studied at the University of Liege in what is now Belgium, and loved the architecture he saw there.

Chávarri was a major entrepreneur and businessman in the Basque region. He was involved in the construction of the Concordia Station which you saw earlier.

Now look carefully at the windows and you will see that every set is different.

Map 8.2 – Return to the centre of the square and stand with Gran Via directly behind you and the Chávarri Palace in front of you.

Turn left to spot the Hotel Carlton – walk towards it.

Hotel Carlton

The Hotel Carlton is a luxury hotel, and inside it has a beautiful Great Oval Hall called Salon La Cristelara. It is covered by an enormous leaded glass dome which was restored in 2007.

During the Spanish Civil war, the Basque government sheltered from the bombs in the basement of the hotel. If you look carefully, you can still see ventilation vents on the steps in front of the hotel entrance.

Map 8.3 – Facing the Carlton, turn right to reach the next building, the Delegación De Hacienda

Delegación De Hacienda

This is the Treasury.   It was built by the Franco government and it was built to intimidate. It was originally crowned with an eagle, the symbol of the fascists, shown above.

There is now a law in Spain requiring all symbols of the Franco regime to be removed. This one survived a long time, but finally it was removed in 2007. They removed it quite neatly, but it must be said that it now just looks like something is missing.

Floral Tribute

Look at the top of the Treasury building again. Note the two twirling sculptures on either side of the space where the eagle and coat of arms was. Now turn round and look at the little flowerbed behind you and which faces towards the building – it is shaped and filled with different coloured flowers to match the twirl.

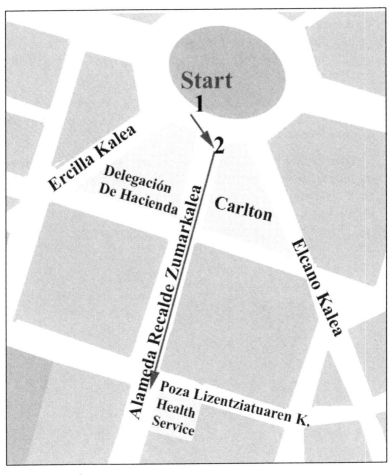

Map 9

Map 9.1 - Face the treasury building again and go down the left-hand side on Alameda Recalde Zumarkalea.

Map 9.2 - Walk along two blocks and you will see the most unusual Health Service building in Europe. It sits on the corner of Alameda Recalde Zumarkalea and Poza Lizentziatuaren Kalea.

The Health Service

Its exterior is covered in mirrored shards, all lying at odd angles and reflecting the surrounding buildings in an unsettling way.

It's ironic that it's actually on the same street as the Casa Montero which is all curves – the complete opposite in design.

Believe it or not, this area has an urban code on new buildings to ensure they fit into their surroundings! The architect fulfilled all the conditions but still managed to create this extraordinary building.

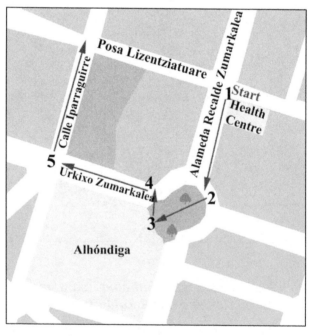

Map 10

Map 10.1 - Continue along Alameda Recalde Zumarkalea to the reach the next roundabout - it is full of trees and little hedges. Diagonally right you will see the Alhóndiga.

Alhóndiga

This building was originally a wine store which as you can see was built with style. It closed in 1970 as a bigger warehouse had been built and this lovely building was abandoned for many years.

The site was later a contender as a location for the Guggenheim museum, but as you know, the Guggenheim was finally sited near the river.

So that left the question on what to do with this building. It was saved from demolition and redesigned by Philippe Starck, and it eventually reopened as a Culture and Leisure centre

Map 10.2 - Cross the little roundabout to enter the Alhóndiga.

Only the exterior was actually preserved, the interior was completely and dramatically replaced. Inside, you will find that the ground floor contains only 43 columns which hold up the rest of the building. The columns are decorated in very individual different ways.

Upstairs there are theatres, a library, restaurants and even a swimming pool which you can see from the ground floor through a glass ceiling.

It's touted as one of the sights to see in Bilbao, but personally I found it disappointingly gloomy inside. So cross the little roundabout to pop in and make up your own mind.

Map 10.3 - When you exit the Alhóndiga turn left to return to the pavement.

Map 10.4 - Turn left again to walk along Urkixo Zumer kalea; the Alhóndiga will be on your left-hand side. You will reach a crossroads.

Map 10.5 - Turn right along Calle Iparraguirre and pass a modern plaza on your right. You will reach a crossroads with Posa Lizentziatuare.

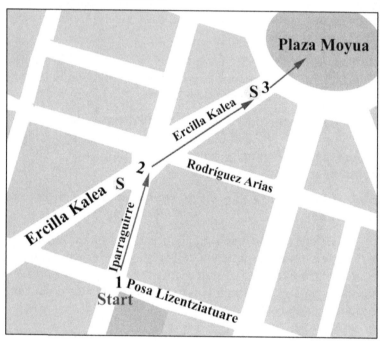

Map 11

Map 11.1 - Cross over and continue straight ahead to reach the next crossroads.

On your left is pedestrianised Ercilla Kalea which welcomes you with a group of three odd statues.

Meninas

These statues were inspired by the famous painting "Meninas" by Velazquez which is in the Prado Museum in Madrd.

It's done with humour and shows two Queen Marianas and one Infanta Margarita, all wearing very wide skirts which was the fashion of the time.

This is the original painting:

Map 11.2 – Stand with the Meninas behind you and face the crossroads.

Directly opposite you is the tree-lined continuation of Ercilla Kalea. Use the two zebra crossings on your right to reach it.

Map –Walk along Ercilla Kalea towards Plaza Moyua once again.

At the end of Ercilla Kalea you will find a statue of José Antonio Aguirre y Lecube.

José Antonio Aguirre y Lecube

He was a footballer who played for Athletic Bilbao, but was best known as President of the first Basque Government.

General Franco forced Aguirre and all of his government into exile and he was never able to return to his country. He died in Paris in 1960.

Map 11.3 - Cross over to return to Plaza Moyua.

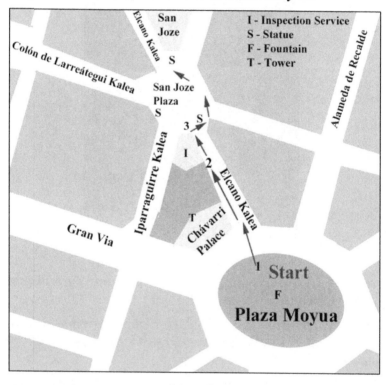

Map 12

Map 12.1 - Orientate yourself once more by locating the oldest-looking building on the Plaza - the Chávarri Palace.

Walk down Elcano Kalea, which is on the right-hand side of Chávarri Palace.

Chávarri Palace Tower

You will first pass a pretty fenced off garden. If you look through the fence back to the Chávarri Palace, you can see its gorgeous tower which is quite hidden from view from the front.

At the end of Elcano Kalea you will see a colourful building on your left with flags flying above a door.

Links with Spain

It's the home of the

High State Inspection Service
in the Basque Autonomous Community

Like many regions in Spain, the Basque region held a number of "Fueros", dating from as far back as the eighth century. A Fuero was a regional law or custom which all Spanish rulers acknowledged and honoured until as late as the nineteenth century.

You will remember the statue of US president John Adams which you saw earlier. He saw the Fueros as an example of how the US constitution could deal with the laws and customs of the various US states.

In the nineteenth century the monarchy and successive governments started to chip away at the Feuros of the Basque Region, and they were finally abolished by General Franco.

When Franco died democracy returned to Spain, and in 1979 the Basques were granted the Statute of Autonomy of Geurnica.

143

The Basques regained part of their independence from Spain, and this building houses one of the administrative links which co-ordinates between The Basque Region and Spain.

Map 12.2 - A few more steps will take you onto busy San Jose Plaza.

Bronze statues and San Joze Plaza

If you look around the plaza you will spot three large metallic statues. They were put there to commemorate the designers and builders of the Ensanche district which you are standing in now.

Across the plaza stands the white San Joze church which the square is named after.

Map 12.3 Use the zebra crossings to reach the front of the church and you can take a closer look at the bronze statues as you do.

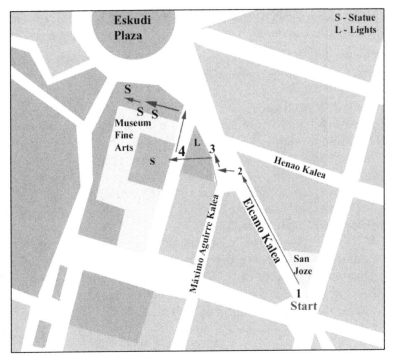

Map 13

Map 13.1 – Face the church door and walk down the left-hand side of the church, still on Elcano Kalea.

In the distance you will see the Iberdrola Dorrea which is the tallest building in Bilbao.

You will reach a junction where Elcano Kalea merges with Máximo Aguirre Kalea.

Map 13.2 - Use the zebra crossings on your left to cross the junction. Turn right to walk towards the rather eccentric Streetlight Garden on your left.

If you visit this area at night you get to see all the streetlights lit up.

Map 13.3 - Follow the path on your left just before the streetlight garden.

The path will take you to the little courtyard in front of the Museo de Belles Artes entrance.

Melpomene Again

Before you go into the museum have a look at another Melpomene statue. This one offended the locals with its nudity and was placed in the archive for nearly thirty years before resurfacing. While it was in seclusion, its place was taken by the more modest statue which you saw on walk 1.

Museo de Belles Artes

Now if you were a bit bemused by the Guggenheim exhibits, this may be more to your liking. The Guggenheim Museum wins on appearance, but this one wins on content. The museum has a really interesting permanent collection and often has an exhibition as well.

It was founded in 1908, although this building was erected after the Spanish Civil War. The permanent collection has pieces from the 12th century up to the present day with 20th century pop art. At the time of writing, the exhibits are arranged in chronological order as you climb the floors.

The museum has a recommended itinerary around the collection which is worth following to get the most out of it in limited time. There is also an audio guide.

Some favourites to find are:

El Greco – The Annunciation

The annunciation is the moment when the Archangel Gabriel broke the good news to Mary that she is going to be the mother of the son of god. He even told her to name her son Jesus, which means Saviour.

El Greco's paintings are always hauntingly colourful, with strangely elongated figures – as is this one.

Martin de Vos – The rape of Europa

This painting tells the story of Europa, a Phoenician woman who took Zeus's fancy.

He turned himself into a handsome white bull, and when Europa climbed on his back he took his chance, and whisked her away to Crete where she became queen. Zeus celebrated all this by putting the constellation Taurus (the bull) in the skies.

Joaquín Sorolla – Kissing the Relic

This painting shows a very strict and forbidding priest allowing the very humble and obedient peasant women to see and kiss a relic.

Ignacio Zuloaga - Portrait of the Countess Mathieu de Noailles

The Countess was a Romanian writer and poet who was part of the intellectual and artistic elite of the day, including Proust.

She was an intelligent, beautiful, striking, and liberated woman and was often painted by the best artists of the time. She was even sculpted by Rodin and the bust is in the New York Met.

She was buried in the Pere Lachaise cemetery in Paris.

Orazio Gentileschi - Lot and his daughters

This painting shows Lot and his daughters, having just escaped from the destruction thrown onto Sodom by God. Of course his wife didn't make it, as she couldn't resist turning round to have a look, I mean who wouldn't?

Seeing what they thought was the end of the world, his daughters decided it was their job to repopulate the world. As the only man left was their father, they got Lot drunk and tricked him into getting them pregnant.

Map 13.4 - Once you have had enough fine art, return to the open air and turn left to walk past the Streetlight Garden to reach the building's much prettier front.

Eve and Risveglio

The two statues flanking the door are by Nemesio Mogrobejo Abásalo who came from Bilbao. He was inspired by Rodin after attending an exhibition of Rodin's works in Paris.

The graceful female statue is Eve, the first woman; her companion however is not Adam, it is Risveglio. The name means awakening and depicts a Revenant, a being from folklore who died and then years later came back to life.

The statues are reproductions and you might already have spotted the originals inside the museum as you explored.

Face the steps and door of the museum. Turn right to walk alongside the building.

Ignacio Zuloaga

You will reach a statue of Ignacio Zuloaga. He was well known for painting bullfighters and gypsies and other Spanish stereotypes. But he also painted the wonderful "Portrait of the Countess Mathieu de Noailles" which you will have admired if you toured the museum.

You have now reached the end of this walk.

Did you enjoy these walks?

I do hope you found these walks both fun and interesting, and I would love feedback. If you have any comments, either good or bad, please review this book

You could also drop me a line on my amazon web page.

Printed in Great Britain
by Amazon